Brew It!

Edited by

Cory Hershberger

Brew It!

Project Team
Editor: Amy Deputato
Copy Editor: Joann Woy
Design: Mary Ann Kahn
Index: Elizabeth Walker

i-5 PUBLISHING, LLC™
Chairman: David Fry
Chief Financial Officer: David Katzoff
Chief Digital Officer: Jennifer Black-Glover
Chief Marketing Officer: Beth Freeman Reynolds
Marketing Director: Will Holburn
General Manager, i-5 Press: Christopher Reggio
Art Director, i-5 Press: Mary Ann Kahn
Senior Editor, i-5 Press: Amy Deputato
Production Director: Laurie Panaggio
Production Manager: Jessica Jaensch

Library of Congress Cataloging-in-Publication Data
Hershberger, Cory, author.
 Brew it! : 25 great recipes and techniques to brew at home / Cory
Hershberger.
    pages cm
 ISBN 978-1-62008-135-8 (paperback)
 1. Beer. 2. Brewing--Amateurs' manuals. I. Title.
 TP577.H459 2015
 641.87'3--dc23
                        2015030605

This book has been published with the intent to provide accurate and
authoritative information in regard to the subject matter within. While every
precaution has been taken in the preparation of this book, the author and
publisher expressly disclaim any responsibility for any errors, omissions,
or adverse effects arising from the use or application of the information
contained herein.

i-5 Publishing, LLC™
www.facebook.com/i5press
www.i5publishing.com

Printed and bound in China
18 17 16 15   2 4 6 8 10 9 7 5 3 1

Contents

Introduction

You're ready to take the home-brewing plunge: you've frequented your local breweries and sampled all of the beers they have to offer, you've chatted up bartenders and the workers at your local liquor store, and you've done preliminary research on ingredients, equipment, and brewing styles. Maybe you're just a burgeoning beer fan who's looking for a new hobby, and you've heard so much about this whole home-brewing thing that you've decided to give it a shot. Or maybe you're somewhere in between: you know the difference between an India pale ale (IPA) and a porter, but you're still a little green about home brewing.

Regardless of where you find yourself on the spectrum, this book will show you that home-brewed bottles of your own endlessly customizable beer are well within your reach. It'll take you through every step of the process, from choosing a style to brew and getting your hands on the necessary equipment to the excitement of brewing day and cracking open that very first bottle of home brew. It's designed to be your constant companion, giving you background info on the history of beer itself, strategies on tweaking and adjusting your batches and recipes to get the exact beer you want, and advice on branding your beers and taking your hobby to the next level, all while incorporating practical tips from other home brewers around the country.

As far as hobbies go, home brewing is pretty inexpensive and one of the best ways to make friends that I've encountered. What better way to break the ice at a party than by bringing a six-pack of your own home-brewed witbier? As long as you keep sanitization your primary concern, the hardest part of home brewing is the waiting. Only brewing day and bottling day require hands-on activity; otherwise, time is the only thing keeping you from cracking open a cold one of your very own.

The groundwork of home brewing is pretty easy to master, but once you've gotten a few batches under your belt, there are a number of additional steps you can take to continue enhancing your creations, including dry-hopping, sparging, and all-grain brewing. This book will focus mainly on brewing with extracts, but I encourage you to try your hand at some of the advanced steps once you're comfortable; they can take your brews to the next level, and experimentation with hop and yeast varieties is half the fun.

Home brewing may be a relatively easy project to tackle, but make sure you've researched well before diving in. You don't want to spend money on batch ingredients only to have them go to waste because you aren't fully prepared for brewing or bottling day. *Brew It!* will take the confusion out of home brewing and equip you with the strategies and skills you need to create your very own beers in the comfort of your home. Best yet, after reading this book, you'll understand the why behind the how, and you'll be able to apply this knowledge to your own recipe adaptation and development.

The History of Beer

It may not be as exciting as getting into the nitty-gritty of brewing beer, but beer's long and storied history is worth more than a glance. It's incredible to see just how far back the beverage dates and to explore how we've arrived where we are today. Beer is tied to the world's economic development as well as to continued scientific discovery. And to think it probably all began by accident!

The Power of Fermentation

It's impossible to know when that inaugural vessel of beer was produced, but it seems likely that it happened— potentially by accident—alongside one of mankind's early attempts at farming cereal. It's even possible that beer was developed before bread through accidental fermentation. Perhaps a farmer allowed some barley to get wet and discovered several days later that it had undergone a change; after tasting the resulting mush, he licked his lips in satisfaction and dove in for more. (Remember, wasting food has only recently become a luxury: in the past, unless you were positive that a food was going to make you sick, you probably ate it.)

Suppositions aside, what we know for sure from pottery and tomb inscriptions is that five millennia ago, brewing beer was a common practice in the ancient civilizations of Sumer and Egypt. As Egyptologists Robert M. Brier and Hoyt Hobbs comment in their book *Daily Life of the Ancient Egyptians* (Greenwood), "Whether beer was first brewed in Sumer or Egypt is still argued—the timing was close, whichever country won the race." The earliest confirmed brewing that we're currently aware of took place around 3500 BC in an ancient Sumerian trading post called Godin Tepe—archaeologists found brewing residue on the inside of a ceramic pot. (Godin Tepe also holds the distinction of being one of the first places in which scientists have found chemical evidence for wine production, too; those ancient Sumerians knew how to party!)

One of the earliest written references to beer is the "Hymn to Ninkasi," a poem found on a clay tablet that dates back to 1800 BC. Ninkasi was the ancient Sumerian goddess of beer, and she was said to

make the beer every day by baking grains in a massive oven, soaking them in water, and then spreading the "wort" out onto mats to dry. In fact, the unknown author of the hymn closes the worship by saying that when Ninkasi pours the filtered beer out of the collection vat, "it is [like] the onrush of the Tigris and Euphrates." Now that's a simile I can get behind!

The hymn actually serves as an early recipe for beer as well. In the 1990s, Fritz Maytag from Anchor Brewing paired up with Dr. Solomon Katz of the University of Pennsylvania, and they set about recreating the Ninkasi brew by following the steps the author laid out. The process looks nothing like what we know today, but the basic

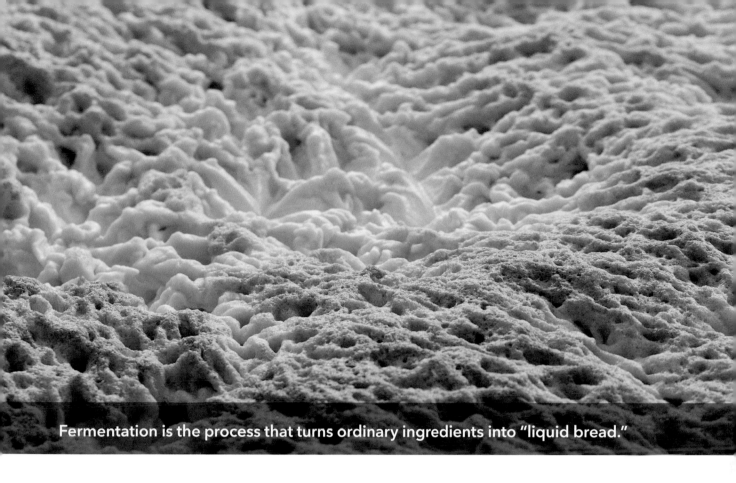

Fermentation is the process that turns ordinary ingredients into "liquid bread."

science was in place. The pair produced a 3.5-percent ABV (alcohol by volume) brew by the end of their experiment, cooling it naturally and drinking it in the traditional Sumerian style: through long straws out of large clay pots. (Straws were commonly used in Sumer because beer produced via this method was often thick and porridge-like, and the straw helped the drinker avoid some of the bitter solids on top of the brew.)

Beer was more than just a pleasant diversion to these ancient civilizations—it was vital to everyday life. The world's first recorded laws, the Code of Hammurabi, state that every citizen was entitled to a daily ration of beer, and the amount depended on social status. Additionally, the Code governed how much tavern keepers could charge for their offerings and also prohibited priestesses of the day from drinking in common taverns—they were welcome to partake, as beer was considered a gift from the gods, but they were required to do it in a sacred manner befitting their holy roles.

Before long, there was no shortage of beer-producing cultures in the ancient world. Just about the only requirement was an agricultural-based society that existed in an environment suitable for the growing of cereal grains. If these relatively simple conditions were met, then beer often followed suit. Because of beer's dependence on cereals for production, civilizations such as ancient Greece preferred wine to beer because the geography lent itself better to the cultivation of grapes and other fruits. Other ancient civilizations, such as Rome, continued to prefer wine even after being introduced to beer—the Roman historian Tacitus wrote disapprovingly of the sour beers of the Germanic tribes of his day in 98 AD: "[They] serve an extract of barley and rye as a beverage that is somehow adulterated to resemble wine." More beer for the rest of us, then!

Nor did beer brewing remain the sole property of Europe and the Middle East. In the Americas, the Inca people brewed a corn-based version of beer that they called *chicha*. In his book *The Inca World* (Anness), David M. Jones explains that chicha was fermented for just a few days to create a weak form to use as a basic daily beverage but that "longer fermentation produced stronger chicha for religious use." In the Far East, Chinese rice farmers experimented with a rice-based alcoholic beverage with at least some similarities to beer. Basically, fermentables of all types and varieties were thriving across almost all cultures as societies continued to grow and multiply.

From Hops and Beyond

We talk about home brewing now as a novel activity, one that brings a predominantly commercial activity into our homes, but, during the Middle Ages, brewing was almost entirely done at home. Commercial breweries as we know them today didn't come about until the eleventh century—in fact, the world's first commercial brewery is widely considered to be the Bavarian State Brewery Weihenstephan in Bavaria, Germany, attached to the Weihenstephan Abbey and licensed in 1040.

Partially because of the small scale of home breweries, the taste of beer was hardly consistent for those first few thousand years of production, both from batch to batch and brewer to brewer. Flavoring agents and ingredient lists weren't set in stone, and properly developed styles as we know them today were still quite a way off. Brewers commonly used an herb-and-spice mix called *gruit* to season and flavor their creations. The specifics of gruit varied between brewers and communities, but it generally contained bitter, woodsy herbs like bog myrtle, yarrow, heather, horehound, juniper, and wild rosemary as well as

Yarrow, a common flavoring in early brews, imparts a bittersweet taste.

Barley has always been beer's main grain.

some types of conifers, fruits, honey, and dates, according to the German Beer Institute. (The term "gruit" also refers to a beer made with gruit as the bittering agent.) Some brewers even treated their specific gruit mixes as trade secrets, keeping them close to their chests.

With the advent of hops as the primary bittering agent in beers all across the world, gruit eventually went out of style; however, some craft breweries, including Beau's All Natural Brewing in Vankleek Hill, Ontario, and Cambridge Brewing in Cambridge, Massachusetts, are experimenting with the style again, releasing seasonal gruit ales and specialty brews all year round. There's even an International Gruit Day every February to celebrate this ancient style of beer. Everything old is new again, right?

Speaking of hops, this modern beer essential that King Henry VIII supposedly called a "wicked and pernicious weed" was not actually documented in the brewing process until the twelfth century, and, considering that beer has been around for millennia, hops are relatively new players to the game. They may have been a part of some brewers' gruit mixes, but hops were not the primary bittering agent in beer until the thirteenth century, when gruit was slowly phased out, beginning in the southern and eastern parts of Europe and ending in England a few hundred years later.

Not only did the inclusion of hops in brewing add the specific bitter taste we recognize today, it aided in preservation, allowing beers to have a much longer shelf life than was possible with gruit. By 1100, large-scale commercial beer brewing was getting its start in Germany (and the German brewers were perhaps beginning to secretly experiment with lagers, according to *World Book Online*), and the year 1632 saw the opening of the first commercial brewery in North America. By this time, hops were forever ingrained in the brewing process, and, today, hops are synonymous with yeast, barley, and water as the main ingredients in beer.

In fact, in 1516, one of the world's oldest food-safety laws, the Bavarian Law of Purity, or the *Reinheitsgebot*, was passed, limiting all beer produced in the German province of Bavaria to the use of only three ingredients: barley, hops, and water. (They wouldn't know about the presence or the importance of yeast for hundreds of years, so beers of the past were fermented with wild yeast found in the air.)

"The intent of the law was to keep beer 'pure' by feudal decree, that is, to keep cheap and often unhealthy ingredients—such as rushes, roots, mushrooms, and animal products—out of the people's drink," writes the German Beer Institute on its website. "In medieval times, brewers often used such ingredients to raise their profits by lowering their standards." This law proved so successful and popular that it existed for almost 500 years, only being struck down in 1987 by the European Court as a restriction on free trade.

Beer for All Ages

As you can see, beer has been regularly consumed by many cultures and by people of all social standings throughout its history. From the farmers who grew the grain to the elite who paid them for it, beer was a key slice of life, and this can be chalked up to a number of reasons. For one thing, during the thousands of years in which food preservation was limited, beer offered a generally safer alternative to plain water for longer term storage. In situations in which water sanitation was poor, beer offered a clean alternative— at least partially due to the high temperatures required during

In the days of the Mayflower, beer was a staple of a nutritious diet.

The Miller Brewing Company was founded in Milwaukee in 1855.

the boiling stage. Without realizing it, centuries of beer brewers were killing bacteria in the water and creating a safer beverage for consumption, with the alcohol content acting as a natural preservative. And it tasted great!

The nutritional value of beer—it has sometimes been referred to as "liquid bread"—also played a role. Beer contains carbohydrates, sugars, and vitamins, all of which have been used throughout history as supplementary nutrition for sailors, monks, farmers, and others. Plus, in situations where food was scarce, being able to get nutrition from your beverage of choice was an important part of staying alive.

Historically, beer has been consumed by people of all ages, including children. On the walls of one ancient Egyptian child's tomb from around 2300 BC, a memorable statement proclaims that the child shall receive, among other things, "a thousand [containers] of beer." While this apparent exaggeration is surely symbolic—and part of the ancient Egyptians' religious beliefs—it does reflect the fact that beer was a common component of children's diets.

Childhood beer consumption was not limited to ancient times. *Small beer*, a.k.a. beer with a low alcohol content, was used throughout history by many families, from medieval village peasants to European families crossing the Atlantic on the Mayflower.

Remember how storms drove the Mayflower north so that it landed in Massachusetts instead of Virginia? The Pilgrims chose not to continue to Virginia because they were out of beer, a supply considered essential because of its stability and nutritional value, according to David M. Keifer in his article "Brewing: A Legacy of Ancient Times." Clearly, in the historical context, beer was not consumed for recreation or for its alcohol content but simply for hydration and as backup in times of poor water. Now, we're lucky enough to live in a culture where we can enjoy the various beer styles at our own leisure, not as a survival necessity. (Though I imagine that some home brewers and craft-beer connoisseurs wouldn't be upset by having to drink only beer for the rest of their lives...)

Regulations

The right to brew your own beer at home for personal consumption–a.k.a., home brewing–has not always been granted to American citizens. Even after the Prohibition Act was repealed in the 1930s, home brewing remained illegal. In fact, it didn't become legal on a federal level until President Jimmy Carter signed an amendment in 1979.

Today, home brewing is legal in all fifty states but regulated on the state level, and laws vary from state to state. The wording of the regulations also varies: for example, in some states, it's legal to transport and serve home-brewed beer to others at certain events, while other states limit the sharing of home brew. In any case, selling bottles of home brew is not allowed; you have to be an operating commercial brewery for that.

Variations

Today, when the casual North American beer drinker—the kind who might keep the occasional six-pack in the fridge for neighborhood get-togethers—thinks of "beer," he or she most likely thinks of the classic American lager. Cold, crisp, and clean with a pale yellow color, these are the beers made famous by brands like Budweiser, Pabst Blue Ribbon, Miller, and others. But lagers are a relatively new development, in widespread use since only about the 1850s, says beer producer Budweiser on its website, **www.budweiser.com**.

Prior to that (and that's several thousand years prior!), ales were the only option. It's suspected that the lager process was "discovered" (and kept a secret) at a much earlier time by attempting to store beer in cold caves, writes The Olde Mecklenburg Brewery on its website (**www.oldemeckbrew.com**), but it wasn't until reliable refrigeration processes were developed in the mid-nineteenth century that lagers could be produced in more locations and during all seasons of the year. After this technological advance, lagers became widely distributed.

In recent years, with the advent of the American craft beer movement and our societal refocus on varied beer types, ales are coming back into style, especially the aggressive types, including India pale ales (IPAs) and imperial stouts. However, despite the number of hipsters you may see twirling their mustaches and sipping craft beer out of a can, small-batch brews still make up less than 5 percent of the total amount of beer sold in America—the macrobreweries still have a corner on the market.

The Prohibition Era

Although not specific to beer alone, you can't discuss the history of beer—at least in the United States—without at least touching on the Prohibition Era, that fascinating thirteen-year period during which a Constitutional amendment made it against federal law to produce, sell, or transport alcohol. Although the good intentions were there—a decrease in crime and alcoholism were expected—the "experiment"

The mayor of Zion City, Illinois, in the process of destroying 80,000 bottles of beer due to Prohibition.

actually resulted in more crime and excess governmental regulation, writes Jennifer Rosenberg for About.com, partly because the amendment tended to make a "criminal" out of the average American.

Much can be said about the Prohibition Era's "speakeasies" (secret bars), gangsters, and rumrunners, but truly, the black-and-white photographs from the 1930s tell the whole story. From policemen dumping barrels of raided bootlegged liquor down a sewer to dozens of men surrounding a gigantic "WE WANT BEER!" sign, it takes only a few minutes of browsing such images to understand the hysteria, the conflicting opinions, and the unintended consequences of one of the United States' most interesting—and temporary—noble experiments.

This is only a mere surface-scratching of beer's storied and valuable history. Entire textbooks have been written about the economic importance and vital presence of this simple fermented beverage throughout the world's development. All I really want to get across to you, fellow home brewer or home brewer-in-training, is that you are the next in line. These age-old traditions are going to continue with you. Ninkasi's blessings on us all!

Get Ready for Brewing

We've covered history, and you've got a grasp on the background of beer brewing, so now it's time to delve into the stuff you came here for: the meat and potatoes of how to brew your own beer at home. This whole process will be detailed in the chapters that follow, but before we discuss the differences between hop strains and the pros and cons of a secondary fermentation, let's go over the basic steps to give you an idea of what you're in for.

There are five basic steps to the home-brewing process: mashing your grains, boiling your wort, chilling your wort, fermenting your brew, and bottling the beer. Thankfully, all of them are pretty simple.

Star San is an effective no-rinse cleaning solution for your equipment.

But First: Cleaning and Sanitizing

Properly cleaning and sanitizing all of your equipment isn't technically a step in the home-brewing process, but it is absolutely vital to making a drinkable batch of beer, and you'll hear it trumpeted throughout the pages of this book. One simple slip-up can ruin your entire home brew before it ever gets a chance to become the beer it was destined to be, so err on the side of caution constantly. Don't ever dunk any unsanitized equipment into your wort or your beer, and make sure that you keep your solution shielded from the air whenever possible. You may feel like you're being overly cautious, but that should be your default state when home brewing—the presence of bacteria may not completely ruin your batch, but it can add unpleasant off-flavors or keep the yeast from working properly in the fermentation and carbonation stages.

Two of the most common sanitizing solutions are the acid blend Star San and iodine. Both of these are no-rinse, meaning that you can soak equipment in the solution and then immediately put it to use, which is incredibly handy. Another common sanitizer in home brewing is bleach, which works in a pinch, but your equipment will need to soak longer in a bleach solution to be sanitary, and you'll need to rinse your equipment exceptionally well once you've finished soaking.

If you make minor mistakes in the other steps, you'll still produce a tasty, drinkable beer, but if you don't clean and sanitize properly, you're just hamstringing yourself right off the bat. When in doubt, sanitize. Your beer (and by extension, your future self and your friends and family) will thank you.

The Five Basic Steps
Mashing

First on the list is mashing, which involves steeping grains in hot—but not boiling—water. This converts the starches in the grains, usually malted barley and occasionally wheat, into sugars that the yeast you add later can process into alcohol. The grain-flavored tea you create in this step is known as *wort*—

you'll hear this word often throughout the book. Mashing is an essential step for proper fermentation later.

Boiling

Once you've brewed your grain tea, it's time to add hops and boil the mixture. Boiling is a vital step because it sanitizes your wort and concentrates the sugars, allowing the yeast to better do its job a few steps down the road. Plus, boiling the wort extracts the acids and oils from the flavoring components—namely hops—that you add, as well as from any other fruits, herbs, and spices that you throw in.

You'll typically boil for an hour, and you'll add hops at three separate times: once to offset the malt's sweetness and make the wort bitter, once for flavor, and once for aroma. Bittering hops go in first, at the start of the boil, followed by flavoring hops toward the end of the hour and finishing with aroma hops at the end of the boil. If you're adding additional flavoring ingredients, they'll go into the wort at the end of the boil, too.

Chilling

When you hit the end of your boil, you'll want to pull the brew kettle off the heat and cool it down to room temperature as quickly as you can so you can add the yeast to your wort. Yeast strains are temperature-rated, meaning that they will work properly only within a specific temperature range, and boiling-hot wort will kill any yeast it comes into contact with. Rapid chilling is desirable because the sooner you're able to get your beer into an airtight fermentor, the safer you'll be—continued exposure to air means continued risk of bacterial contamination. On a related note, everything that touches your wort after you stop the boil must be sanitized. Everything.

There are two primary ways to rapidly cool your wort: an ice bath or a device called a wort chiller. The ice bath is just what it sounds like: you set

Remember the Basics

Say it with me: mash your grains, boil and chill your wort, ferment, and bottle your beer. If you get those five steps down, you can handle whatever tweaks and turns a recipe will add to the process. There are certainly substeps and variations involved in home brewing, but that's what the rest of this book is for. Let's dive in.

the (covered) brew kettle into a sink or bathtub filled with ice and water and wait until your temperature falls into the desirable range. Wort chillers work much faster and cool by either running the wort through chilled piping or running cold water through piping that is set down into the hot wort. As you're chilling, whichever method you choose, try not to disturb the kettle too much because letting it sit calmly allows the existing sediment—proteins, hop and grain residue, and the like—to settle to the bottom. This gunk is called *trub*.

After your wort has reached room temperature (or whatever temperature your yeast strain requires), you'll need to transfer the liquid into a sanitized fermenting vessel. You can choose either a fermenting bucket or a carboy, the latter of which is a glass or plastic jug.

Fermenting

Now that your wort is a satisfactory temperature and you've transferred it to your fermentor, you need to stir in, a.k.a. *pitch*, the yeast to get the mixture to ferment. Fermentation is essential to the beer-making process because the yeast transforms the sugars in your wort into ethanol molecules, causing the beer to become alcoholic and giving it the

Adding, or "pitching," the yeast starts the fermentation process.

trademark flavor we all know and love. During this process, the yeast will give off carbon dioxide, which will escape your fermentor via the airlock; once these bubbles stop, the fermentation has completed. Optionally, you can choose to do a secondary fermentation, which helps clarify your beer and adds additional aged flavors; however, this is only really required with a handful of beer styles, including barleywines and lagers. (See Chapter 7, Beer Styles, for more information.)

Primary fermentation (for most styles of beer) will finish up in about a week. When the yeast falls to the bottom of the fermentor, a.k.a. flocculates, it has finished processing the sugar in the wort, and the beer is ready to drink—flavor-wise, anyway. It's not carbonated, but that's what the final step will achieve.

Bottling

The aforementioned steps all take place on the same day, aptly named brew day; bottling is the only step that takes place on a separate day. Guess what it's called? Yep: bottling day. You'll need to siphon your beer with a spigot from its fermenting vessel into a bottling bucket, mix in some additional sugar—this is called *priming sugar* and is typically added as part of a simple syrup—and transfer it to your bottles. Commercial breweries force-carbonate their beer by mixing it with carbon dioxide as they bottle it, but home brewers take advantage of the remaining yeast cells in the beer and let the carbonation happen naturally. That's where the priming sugar comes into play: as the yeast acts on this sugar in a sealed vessel, the carbon dioxide can't escape, resulting in beer's refreshing fizz.

On bottling day, you bottle and cap your home brew.

The Ingredients

How can just a handful of innocuous ingredients produce the delicious ales, porters, lagers, and stouts that we love so much? Water, grain, malt, hops, and yeast—along with some tasty enhancements—come together and, after some microbiology magic, transform into that golden nectar appreciated by centuries of beer drinkers.

Before diving into home brewing proper, it helps to understand what these ingredients are and what roles each play in beer production. Let's get to know these key players a little better.

Water

Whether you use city water from a tap, well water, or bottled water, the wet stuff—and its makeup—matters. Little changes in water chemistry can make a big difference in the taste of your beer, says Erik Nielsen, co-owner of Two Shy Brewing in Roseburg, Oregon.

"As home brewers, we did a clinic on water and water chemistry," he explains. "We poured beer into tasting glasses, and we sprinkled a little bit of calcium, gypsum, Epsom salts, and baking powder into each one. We were amazed. Depending on the chemistry of the water, the flavor of the beer totally changed."

In general, if your water tastes good, your beer should taste good, says veteran home brewer and author John Palmer from Monrovia, California. If your water doesn't taste so great, you should pretreat it. You can boil it to take out the smell of chlorine, add potassium metabisulfite tablets to remove chlorine and chloramines, use an activated charcoal filtration system to remove dissolved gases and organic substances, or use a water softener to remove minerals.

Nielsen recommends that home brewers test their water to find a pH and mineral-content baseline. "A water test isn't that expensive," he says. "It would be cool for any home brewer to take a sample and get it analyzed so that you know what your starting point is."

Bottled water is an option for brewers with less-than-ideal water, Palmer notes. "It typically has low levels of alkalinity and minerals," he says. "Reverse osmosis and distilled water can be added to your tap water to reduce the mineral levels as necessary."

Of course, all of these steps are for intermediate and advanced home brewers who want as much control as possible over their final product. The best rule of thumb for your first batch is Palmer's: if your water tastes good, your beer should taste good. Even if your water isn't ideally flavored, as long as it is potable and palatable, your final result should be drinkable, at least from a water standpoint. If you're concerned, you can jump into pretreatment options or swapping out tap water for bottled or distilled water.

Good beer starts with good water.

The Grain

In addition to water, the most important ingredient in beer brewing is the grain, according to Nielsen. The barley varieties typically used in beer brewing are two-row and six-row (the names refer to the arrangement of the kernels).

"Barley is beer," Nielsen says. "Barley is the base. It's where you're getting the sugar from. The yeast eats the sugar and produces alcohol. At least 80 percent of your mash will be barley; the other 20 percent is your adjuncts." (For most styles of beer, that is—wheat beers, for instance, have a lower percent of barley and a higher percent of adjuncts, which are non-barley grains.)

Barley is the foundation of a majority of beers.

A member of the grass family, barley is unique in that its husk contains an enzyme that facilitates the breakdown of the grain's sugars, Palmer says. The enzyme is released during the malting process, when the grain is soaked, allowed to partially germinate, and then kiln-dried and/or toasted. "The purpose of malting is to create the enzymes, break down the matrix surrounding the starch granules, prepare the starches for conversion, and then stop this action until the brewer is ready to utilize the grain," Palmer adds.

Brewers use other grains in their beer, too, including wheat, oatmeal, corn, and rice, Nielsen says. These grains are referred to as *adjuncts,* and they add flavor and body to beer, but they don't necessarily contribute starches to the mix. "Adjuncts may or may not have fermentable starches on them, and they do not have a natural enzyme on them to break them down," he explains. "You can get away with brewing an all-corn beer if you want to, but you'd need a synthetic enzyme of some kind to break it down."

The Hops

Fruity, spicy, citrusy, and aromatic, hops impart both bitterness and aroma to beer. A natural preservative, they've been used in brewing for more than 1,000 years. Today, more than 100 hop varieties are available to home brewers—see "Hop Varieties" on page 28 for information on some of the most common types used in home brewing.

"You have a spicy hop, an earthy hop, and a citrus hop," Nielsen says. "And then you have all these cross-varieties, which [result from] mixing and matching and trying to get different flavors and different alpha acids." Hops are divided into two general categories: bittering and aroma. Bittering hops, sometimes called *kettle* hops, are high in alpha-acid resins, while aroma hops, or *finishing* hops, typically have a lower alpha-acid content and contribute a desirable aroma and flavor to the beer, Palmer notes.

"Bittering hops are added at the start of the boil and boiled for about an hour," he says. "Aroma hops are added toward the end of the boil and are typically boiled for 15 minutes or less. By adding different varieties at different times during the boil, a more complex hop profile can be established that gives the beer a balance of hop bitterness, taste, and aroma."

Aroma hops can be further delineated into flavoring and aroma hops, but this distinction refers to when they're added in the boiling process, not differences in their flavors—flavoring hops are added toward the end

Hops come in flower and pellet form.

of the boil to impart their flavor (but not their bitterness) to the wort, whereas aroma hops are added at the very end of the boil to maximize their aroma.

Hops come in whole, pelleted, and plug forms, and each has benefits and drawbacks. Whole hops are easy to strain from the wort, provide great aroma, and are good for dry-hopping, Palmer says. Pellets are easy to weigh and they store well, but they turn into hop sludge at the bottom of the kettle, which can be difficult to strain. Plugs retain freshness, come in convenient ½-ounce units, and behave like whole hops in the wort.

"Whichever you choose, freshness is important," Palmer says. "Fresh hops smell fresh, herbal, and spicy, like evergreen needles, and have a light green color, like freshly mown hay." Beware: If your hops smell like old, musty cheese, they've spoiled. Don't brew with them, or your beer will taste similar, and you definitely don't want that.

The Yeast

In the beer-making process, yeast cells are invaluable little workers that transform sugar into alcohol. In chemistry terms, the yeast cells take in simple sugars, such as glucose and maltose, and then produce carbon dioxide and alcohol as waste products.

Brewers use two main yeast types: ale and lager, Nielsen says. Ale yeasts prefer warmer temperatures, working quickly and going dormant below about 55 degrees Fahrenheit. Lager yeasts like things a little cooler, working more slowly and going dormant at about 40 degrees F.

"The majority of microbrewers use ale yeast," Nielsen notes, "but lager yeasts can give you refreshing, crisp beer with a cleaner flavor."

You can find scores of ale and lager yeast strains, and each one produces a different flavor profile. Some create fruity esters that smell like bananas, and others produce phenols that smell like cloves. Many major breweries have proprietary strains of yeast, Palmer says.

"These yeast strains have evolved with the style of beer being made," he adds. "Yeast readily adapts and evolves to specific brewer conditions, so two breweries producing the same style of beer with the same yeast strain will actually have different yeast cultivars that produce unique beers."

Optional Ingredients

Water, grain, hops, and yeast are the only essential pieces needed to brew beer, but some of the more advanced styles have add-ins outside the scope of the *Reinheitsgebot*, or Bavarian Law of Purity. As a matter of fact, when that law was passed, the existence and necessity of yeast hadn't even been discovered, so the law only required that beer be made from barley, water, and hops.

Clarifying Agents

Clarifiers clear beer that's cloudy from unflocculated (a.k.a. unclumped) yeast, unconverted starch, or residual proteins. These extra ingredients, which are added to your wort and beer, will chemically and electrostatically pull haze-formers out of solution and allow them to settle to the bottom, Palmer says. Irish moss and isinglass are the most common clarifiers used by home brewers.

"Irish moss is a type of red seaweed called *carrageen* that attracts large proteins," Palmer explains. "It's added during the last 20 minutes of your boil, where it greatly enhances the clumping and precipitation of the hot-break proteins that would otherwise contribute to haze and staling reactions."

Isinglass—which is an excellent yeast clarifier—is composed of the protein collagen, and it's obtained by cleaning and drying the swim bladders of fish, Palmer notes. "While it's able to bind and settle some of the larger proteins, it's not very effective for reducing chill haze," he notes. "To use it, add it to the fermentor after fermentation has finished or to the bottling bucket when you add your priming sugar solution."

Other Add-Ins

These items don't serve a specific chemical purpose like the clarifying agents do, but they can take a beer to the next level by bringing additional flavor notes and dimensions to a brew. Some substyles, such as pumpkin ales and winter warmers, wouldn't even exist without additional flavoring ingredients.

A general rule of thumb for adding flavoring ingredients is to use slightly fewer hops than you would normally use because sometimes a gentle flavoring ingredient can be overpowered by the aggressiveness of hops. Those in-your-face flavors are why we love hops so much, of course, but that doesn't mean you want to trump your experimental flavors with them. Keep in mind also that if you're brewing a style with strong flavors on its own—such as an IPA, for example—you'll need a considerable amount of the add-in to properly compete with the beer's flavor.

When you're adding extra ingredients, remember that the later you add in the flavoring agents, the stronger their end flavors will be because less of the flavor will be boiled away. If you want a strongly flavored orange IPA, you should add in your orange peels at *flame out* (the very end of the boil, when

Hop Varieties

There are dozens and dozens (and dozens) of hop varieties available to home brewers today. Although it wouldn't seem that varieties would vary that much because they're all still of the same species–*Humulus lupulus*, to be exact–the opposite is true. Hop types can have notes of mint, citrus, and mango, and can be exceedingly acidic or comparatively basic.

Curious about the different flavors and aromas of these hop varieties? Try them out by brewing hop tea, Nielsen suggests. "Go to brewing-supply store, buy little 2-ounce samples of every hop, steep them into teas, and taste them," he says. "Get to know their smells and their flavors."

The following are some of the most common hops called for in home-brewing recipes–all home-brew supply stores should carry these in pellet form, and stores may be able to order whole hop flowers for you if you'd like. The recommendations on bittering versus aroma hops that follow are just guidelines–if you'd like to use Amarillo hops as bittering hops, go for it. Experiment as you see fit.

Amarillo	Floral and tropical, this type is best used as aroma hops.
Cascade	This is one of the most commonly used American hop varieties, excellent as both an aroma and a bittering hop.
Centennial	Sometimes called "Super Cascade," this variety is like Cascade with the volume knob turned to 11.
Chinook	Best as a bittering variety, this floral, herbal variety is great in pale ales.
Citra	Commonly used in India pale ales (IPAs), this type is best used as an aroma hop so that its strong citrus flavors stay up front in your final beer.
Crystal	Mild and floral, Crystal hops are a nice all-purpose aroma hop variety.
Fuggles	This United Kingdom-grown variety is best as an aroma hop in English beers.
Galena	One of the most widely grown American bittering hops, Galena is excellent as an all-purpose addition.
Hallertau	This go-to hop for an authentic European brew is mildly spicy and best as an aroma hop.
Mosaic	Complex and piney, Mosaic hops lend themselves nicely to IPAs as both a bittering and an aroma choice.
Nugget	Herbal and heavy, Nugget hops are best for their bittering properties.
Simcoe	Piney and resinous, this highly acidic hop can be used as either a bittering or aroma addition.
Summit	Highly acidic, Summit is one of the most aggressive bittering hops available.
Willamette	Mildly bitter and not citrusy, this variety stands out from its fellow American types. It's best as an aroma addition.

you pull your kettle off the heat) or after to get the best flavor; meanwhile, if you want only a hint of maple in your amber ale, you can add some maple earlier in the boil.

Flavor add-ins can be split into the following three primary ingredient types.

Irish moss is a typical additive to clarify the appearance of the finished product.

Herbs and Spices

Similar to how gruit was made before the advent of hops (see "From Hops and Beyond" in Chapter 1), herbs and spices can add welcome complexity to beers, prompting drinkers to ask about the secret ingredient. (That said, there's a common Belgian saying that if you can single out any one spice in a beer, the brewer used too heavy a hand when adding it, so to each his own!)

You should add spices at the same time you add your aroma hops—right before or at flame out. If you boil some of the spices for too long, either they can take on a bitter quality or their delicate flavors will be disguised by the stronger hoppy, malty notes of a beer. Adding the spices at the end preserves their fresh flavors as much as possible in the final product.

The list of possible herbs and spices to try is nearly endless, but for your first bits of experimentation, go for flavors that you know will marry well with beer—vanilla, lemongrass, cinnamon, nutmeg, cloves, and ginger are all excellent beginning points (although admittedly not all at the same time). Winter warmers or holiday ales often have a mix of spices similar to gingerbread or spice cake, and those flavors lend themselves well to a malty amber ale, for instance, while an IPA could benefit from citrusy lemongrass and pungent basil. You could even add galangal and kaffir lime leaves for a Thai-themed IPA (ThaiPA, anyone?).

Fruits and Vegetables

Pumpkin ales and fruity lambics owe their very existence to the fruits and vegetables they're brewed with, and you can create your very own spins on these beer staples by adding fruits and vegetables to all kinds of beer styles. The best way to add the flavors of fresh produce to your beers is in the secondary fermentation process: after primary fermentation is complete, siphon the beer into a clean, sanitized fermentor and then add in your fruits and/or vegetables. This secondary fermentation will allow the flavors of your produce to remain up front in your final product.

As with herbs and spices, the sky's the limit with produce add-ins, but some fruits and vegetables will give you better results than others. Obviously, pumpkin is an extremely common choice, but berries and citrus fruits also work well. (If you do use citrus fruits, remember that the essential oils you're looking for are found in the peel, not in the fruit itself.)

Keep in mind that most of the fruits you'll use in your beers will have some wild yeast left in them, even if they were frozen or pasteurized before use, and sometimes that wild yeast can start a new fermentation process in the secondary fermentor. If this happens, it's no big deal—the biggest concern is that your beer may skew a little sour on the taste spectrum, which is to be expected. The fruit beers

Pumpkin is a popular additive to seasonal autumn brews.

Fruits such as peaches and apricots create sweet, lighter flavors for spring and summer.

you purchase on the market have likely been brewed with fruit syrups and then pasteurized to ensure that the wild yeast can't continue fermentation, but the home-brewing method with whole fruits will produce a slightly different (and in my opinion, better) result.

Sweeteners

Malted barley will provide all of the sugars that your yeast needs to create alcohol, but you can add some additional sweeteners to provide a rounder, deeper flavor for your end product. The aforementioned maple syrup is a good choice, as is a sorghum syrup, especially in Southern states, where it's most popular. Molasses can take a stout or porter to the next level, and using specific varieties of honey can provide completely unique riffs on beer styles—think orange-blossom honey in lighter beers for another dimension of citrus, or wildflower honey for floral notes. (If you do use honey, make sure to add it after the boil has ceased because boiling honey can cause some off-flavors.) You can also use some sweeteners as priming sugars to bottle-condition your beers (see "Priming and Racking Your Beer" in Chapter 6).

Get Creative

Keeping the basic ingredients in mind, don't be afraid to play around with grain-hop-yeast combinations and then try adding some additional flavor add-ins. Follow a basic recipe, gradually learn how to manipulate it, and have fun with your brews, Nielsen says.

"It's OK to switch out ingredients and just experiment," he adds. "Play with it. Look for what's new, try new varieties of hops that are out, and experiment with making teas out of grains and hops."

Additionally, chances are that if you've had a recipe idea for a batch of home-brewed beer, someone else has, too. Do some poking around online to discover if that brussels-sprout pale ale worked for someone else, and, if you're lucky, you may even find a starting point recipe to build from. It's a good idea to check online for recommended amounts of optional flavoring ingredients in a single batch, too. If you're spending the money on the ingredient, you don't want to waste it by purchasing too little or too much, not to mention the fact that different parts of the ingredient may provide better flavor (for instance, the rinds of citrus fruits, as previously mentioned).

Understanding what the ingredients bring to the beer-brewing process is essential to eventually crafting your own recipes. Just tweaking a hop variety here and an add-in there can create an entirely new brew. Now let's get into how these ingredients come together to result in delicious beer.

The Whole Kit and Caboodle

Beer brewing seems overwhelming at first blush, especially if you've ever toured a commercial brewery. Home brewing will always somewhat resemble a science experiment (just wait until that yeast starts working!), but it's not only possible but eminently doable to recreate those commercial setups at home on a (much) smaller scale, especially if you use a starter kit.

Starter kits take most of the confusion out of the brewing process, providing everything you need to successfully create your first batch. Instead of doing extensive research, you can pick up a kit to have the perfect jumping-off point. If you want to continue with home brewing as a serious hobby, you'll probably need to pick up additional equipment to delve into advanced recipes; for example, some require multiple fermentations or temperature-controlled fermentation and storage, both of which are above the purview of a basic kit.

Recipe kits: These include the actual consumable ingredients for your beer. Each recipe kit typically includes fermentables, such as grains or malt extracts, or honey for honey ales; hops; yeast; steeping grains; and priming sugar, as well as a muslin bag to hold your steeping grains. If you're purchasing a specialty beer that requires additional flavoring or coloring agents, those will be included. There are two major types of recipe kits–extract and all-grain–both of which will brew approximately 5 gallons, or 48 12-ounce bottles, of beer.

The major variable for recipe-kit pricing is the style of beer you'll be brewing; anything with additional flavorings or fermentables–think honey ales and double IPAs–will (understandably) cost more. Expect to spend as little as $25 for a simple brown-ale kit and more than $50 for a more complex beer, like a bourbon-barrel porter.

Extract kits: As a beginner, extract kits offer the best way to get your feet wet, and this book advocates that you begin with an extract batch before graduating to an all-grain creation. Extract kits include the same ingredients as an all-grain kit, but the major difference is that the malt extracts are included, thus eliminating the extra steps of mashing and sparging. Because of this, they require less equipment, take less time, and are easier all around for beginner brewers.

All-grain kits: As just mentioned, brewing from all grains–without premade malt extract–requires a few extra steps and more time, but for intermediate home brewers, going all-grain is the natural next step. It's probably wise to get a few batches of extract-based beer under your belt before progressing to an all-grain kit.

Small-batch kits: Some brewing-supply stores and manufacturers sell small-batch kits, which result in only 1 gallon of beer instead of 5 gallons. These small batches of beer are perfect for dabbling in recipe additives once you have a little bit of experience, and the kits are priced accordingly–usually less than $15.

A starter kit is an excellent choice for an initial home-brewing attempt. The included instructions and individually packaged items make things much simpler on brewing and bottling days, and the kits remove much of the guesswork from the process. That said, kits are not for everyone. If you're looking for a customizable home-brewing experience that allows more wiggle room in recipe development, you might be better served by purchasing everything individually, especially if you're looking to continue the hobby beyond a few batches.

If you do decide to pursue recipe development in the future, or you choose to piece together your equipment and ingredients in a more organic fashion, you won't regret the brewing fundamentals you learned from brewing with kits.

Grow Your Own Hops

If you want to take the DIY aspect of home brewing to the next level, try growing hop plants of your very own! Just one plant produces up to 2 pounds of dried hop flowers, called *cones*. You can grow enough hops for your home brew and have plenty to share, too. Growing your hops means you have a fresher ingredient at a much lower price.

Hops thrive in plant hardiness zones 3 through 9, which is almost everywhere in the United States. (You can determine your hardiness zone by viewing the USDA Plant Hardiness Zone Map at http://planthardiness.ars.usda.gov/phzmweb.) Technically, hops are not vines but bines, meaning they climb with their entire stems rather than their leaf tendrils. Join the backyard bine-to-bottle movement by following this easy twelve-step growing program.

1. Select a spot to grow your hops. The location should get more than 8 hours of sun per day, it shouldn't stay soggy, and it must have access to a spigot. Make sure there's room to trellis your hops 12 to 18 feet high but away from power lines. Some home brewers with two-story houses let their beer flags fly—and perhaps annoy their homeowners' associations—by planting hops on the sunny side of their houses. They train the bines on twine running through eyebolts or pulleys mounted under the eaves. The hops get great sun, and the windows are shaded from summer heat.

2. Your local home-brew supply store might sell rhizomes (roots) of female hops plants in the spring. If not, you can find mail-order sources online. Either way, order early before the most popular varieties sell out. Choose varieties developed in the United States and better adapted to our conditions, such as Brewer's Gold, Chinook, Columbus, Galena, Willamette, and Zeus.

3. Get a soil test from your local cooperative-extension office (or office locations, visit www.csrees.usda.gov/extension). Some offices provide soil testing for free or at a low cost. Follow the test's recommendations to get your soil's pH to between 6 and 8 with an application of lime or sulfur.

4. Hops need rich, well-drained soil, so add a bag of compost and a couple of fistfuls of organic fertilizer for each rhizome. Resist the temptation to overdo the fertilizer. Plants that get too much nitrogen (the first of three numbers on the fertilizer's label) are like humans who eat too much sugar: their long-term health suffers.

   Most plant diseases and bug infestations can be traced to a diet too rich in nitrogen. Excess nitrogen also reduces the potency of the cones.

5. In spring, plant the rhizomes at least 42 inches apart. This distance keeps their side branches from entangling and allows enough air circulation to curb foliage diseases. Scoop out a trench 1 to 2 inches deep to set the rhizome in and cover it firmly with soil. Make sure that the white shoots point up and the brown roots point down. Water them in. If you'll be trellising near your house, make sure the beds aren't under the rain shadow of the eaves; you want them to get plenty of rain water.

6. Apply a 2-inch layer of mulch (e.g., bark, wood chips, shredded leaves) to reduce weeds, keep the soil moist, feed worms, and make the bed more attractive. Reapply mulch each fall after cutting the frost-killed bines back to the ground.

7. For each rhizome, attach two lengths of fuzzy twine to a wooden post in the ground or wooden edging. Bailing twine or jute works well and is biodegradable. Run the twine at least 12 to 18 feet high and through an eyebolt or pulley attached to a sturdy trellis (or to the eaves of your house). Hook the twine on a nail or a cleat near the ground so you can lower each bine to the ground for easy harvest in the late summer and fall.

8. When the spring shoots grow 6 to 12 inches high, cut them to the ground except for the two biggest ones. Trellis the two big ones by wrapping them clockwise around the twine. Don't break the tender tip, as that will slow growth considerably. The prunings can be sautéed with butter and garlic for a "poor man's asparagus."

9. Keep plants watered with a soaker hose or drip line. A sprinkler can spread diseases.

10. By summer, prune out any leaves below 2 feet to reduce diseases.

11. About 120 days after the bines have started growing, you can begin harvesting cones (although you might not get a lot the first year). Dry them in a paper bag in a warm, dark room. Store any dried cones that you don't use right away in a dated, vacuum-sealed bag.

12. Celebrate with your first batch of home brew that also tastes of home-grown accomplishment.

Equipment

The equipment you need to brew a batch of beer isn't the star of the show. That role typically falls to the ingredients. Who cares about a sturdy brew kettle or well-designed siphon system when you can watch the colors bloom as you steep grains to create wort or smell the fragrance of hops as they bubble away?

That doesn't make the equipment any less important, though. Consider a brewer's toolbox the chef's knife of the home-brewing world: a delicious, five-star meal starts with a sharp, trusty knife, just like the IPA you're dying to brew starts with reliable equipment.

Brew Day Basics

You can piece together your required equipment à la carte or pick up an equipment kit that will include most, if not all, of everything discussed here. (For information on kits, check out "Equipment Kits" on page 45.) However you choose to obtain it, you'll need all of the following to create your first batch.

Brew Kettle

The backbone of brewing day, the brew kettle or brew pot is where your beer will begin. You'll be creating wort by steeping the grains and adding the malt extract and hops to your water base, all while the mixture bubbles away in your brew kettle. Similar to stockpots, brew kettles come in a variety of shapes and sizes, some with built-in thermometers and/or auto-sparging capacities (sparging is an extra step required during all-grain brewing; see page 52).

If you choose to buy a brew kettle without a thermometer, you will need to purchase a separate thermometer because you must monitor the temperature of the wort throughout brewing. Brew kettles can range in price from $30 to $40 for basic stainless-steel pots and up to $200 and more for larger, more advanced models.

Spoon or Paddle

On a related note, you need a large spoon or brewing paddle—like a canoe paddle with holes in it—to keep the wort moving as it boils. You won't have to stir constantly, but as you add malt extracts, you'll need to keep the viscous liquid from burning to the bottom of the kettle. Make sure that the spoon is large enough to reach the bottom of your brew pot. You can spend less than $5 for a basic plastic spoon or paddle, while stainless-steel models range up to $40.

Fermentor

After brewing your wort and pitching your yeast, you need to move the mixture into a vessel that provides an environment for the yeast to start working. That vessel is called a fermentor, with two Fs and one O (the person doing the fermenting is called a fermenter, with three Es.) Your two main options here are a food-grade plastic bucket, a.k.a. an "ale pail," or a carboy, which looks like a giant bottle with a narrow neck and comes in glass and plastic varieties. Your selection can depend on your budget and the amount of beer you wish to brew. A plastic bucket will cost around $15, while carboys will run $25 to $40, depending on the size and what they are made of.

Carboys are nice because you can see the beer as it ferments, potentially catching any issues early, though they can be heavy and ungainly to move around and store, especially when they're full of fermenting wort. Buckets are much easier to reposition, and they have the added benefit of being cheaper than carboys; however, you're giving up that wort visibility, which is a deal-breaker for some home brewers. If you're still not sure which vessel you'd prefer, Dave Butler, blogger at Fermentedly Challenged, provides a nice breakdown of the pros and cons of each fermenting vessel: www.fermentedlychallenged.com.

You'll need a second vessel to hold your beer for bottling. An ale pail with a spigot attached is the most common choice here. As such, these ale pails are sometimes called bottling buckets.

Airlock

The airlock serves a very important purpose during fermentation, allowing carbon dioxide produced by the fermenting process to escape the fermentor without allowing air to enter, thus preventing bacterial

The brew kettle is where it all begins.

A clear glass or plastic carboy allows you to see the beer as it ferments.

contamination. Airlocks come in two primary designs: the bubbler airlock, which looks like the letter "S" with a few added globes, and a three-piece airlock, which comes standard with most starter kits. All you need to do is fill the airlock with a little distilled water or sanitizing solution and then stick it in the specially designed rubber grommet or bung that comes with it. Science will do the rest. Because it's made of plastic, an airlock will typically cost only a few dollars, grommet and all.

Thermometer

You'll need to keep tabs on the temperature of your wort throughout the brewing process: as you steep your grains, as you cool the wort, and as the wort ferments. It's easiest to accomplish this with two separate thermometers: one that can stick to the outside of your fermentor, sometimes called a *fermometer* (clever, I know), and a portable one that is rated for temperatures above 200 degrees Fahrenheit.

A fermometer is just a simple plastic strip that sticks to the outside of the fermentor and tells you its temperature. It's not high-tech or incredibly accurate, but it gets the job done. A fermometer tells you how warm or cool your fermenting wort is without risking contamination by breaking the seal.

A fermometer usually costs less than $5, and I'd recommend getting one for every fermenting vessel you'll be using.

Monitoring temperatures is essential at various stages of brewing.

You can go the analog or digital route for your portable thermometer. I personally still use a lab thermometer to check wort temperatures, and I've never had any issues with it, but feel free to go the digital route if you'd prefer—the faster readings are a definite plus, although that is offset by the higher cost. Lab thermometers and other nondigital models will run you around $10, while digital varieties cost around $20.

Cleaning and Sanitizing Equipment

As the unsung hero of bottling day, cleaning and sanitizing equipment will keep the beer you've spent so much time brewing unspoiled as it carbonates. You need three specific items: a cleaning solution, a sanitizer, and brushes, all of which will cost less than $10 total.

Cleaning Solution

First, you want to remove any deposits from the bottles and fermentors by using a cleaning solution. Basic mild dish detergent will work. If you have stubborn deposits or buildup, advanced cleaners, such as Powdered Brewing Wash (PBW) and Straight-A Premium Cleanser, should do the trick.

Sanitizer

The cardinal rule of brewing (in my book, anyway) is that sanitization is key. Any object that comes into contact with the wort or the beer after boiling ends has the potential to introduce bacteria into the brew, which can spoil an entire batch. As such, you have to sanitize everything religiously. As previously mentioned, a number of sanitizers are available, including bleach, iodine-based formulas

(such as Iodophor), and Star San, an acid-based sanitizer favored by Northern Brewer Homebrew Supply. Whichever you choose, I'd recommend a no-rinse solution; it's just going to make your life easier in the long run.

Brushes

You'll use brushes to scrub out your fermentor(s) as well as each individual beer bottle, especially if you're reusing bottles from commercial breweries. Any remaining sediment in the bottles can spoil the new beer. You'll find regular bottle-cleaning brushes as well as carboy-cleaning brushes, which have 90-degree bends to clean the upper sides of the carboy.

Bottling Bits
Racking Cane and Tubing

After fermentation is complete, you have to transfer your beer from your primary fermentor to a bottling bucket. You need to do this without introducing a large amount of air into the beer, which is where the racking cane and tubing come into play. The racking cane, a rigid tube with a small inverted tip, attaches to a length of plastic tubing. Using gravity to your advantage, you'll create a miniature vacuum that sucks the beer from your fermentor into your bottling bucket. Seven Bridges Cooperative (www.breworganic.com) has a nice breakdown of how best to siphon your beer; it can be a little tricky to start the process, especially for the first time. A racking cane and siphon tubing will typicall cost $10 or more.

Bottling Wand

Also called a bottling tube, this little gadget is going to be your best friend on bottling day. Attached to the spigot on your bottling bucket, this handy device minimizes the contact your beer will have with the air, thereby minimizing your

A bottle brush bends to reach areas that you can't.

contamination risks. Just lower the tube into the bottle and press the release valve firmly against the bottom. This will cause beer to flow from the bucket into the bottle with ease. To halt the flow, just pull the release valve off the bottom; simple physics and flow mechanics have never been so practical. A bottling wand is included in most starter kits; otherwise, you should buy one on its own.

Bottles

This one is pretty self-explanatory. These glass receptacles hold your delicious home brew in single-serving amounts. You can purchase the bottles new (your best bet for a problem-free batch), or you can reuse commercial brewery bottles, provided they have been cleaned and sanitized thoroughly and feature pry-off, not twist-off, caps. Twist-off bottles tend to be difficult to keep airtight, according to the American Homebrewers Association.

You likely want to start with 12-ounce glass bottles, but you also can use the 22-ounce bottles, called bombers, that typically hold commercial craft beers, or even growlers from your favorite local brewery. You can also use swing-top bottles, which come in sizes that range between 16 and 32 ounces. Keep in mind that if you choose to use larger receptacles, you typically need to drink the beer within a day or two of cracking the seal because the carbonation will weaken with time. If you're brewing a traditional 5-gallon batch of beer, you'll need enough bottles to hold roughly 600 ounces of beer: that's fifty 12-ounce bottles or twenty-three 22-ouncers.

I prefer longnecks and bombers, personally, because they hold small enough amounts of beer that you can easily drink one in a single sitting, they're easy to give to friends and family (because you won't need to hassle with getting the bottles back), and they can be obtained for "free" by saving bottles from commercial six-packs. (Obviously, they're not free, but I like the ability to recycle beer bottles whenever possible.) Swing-top bottles, however, are incredibly easy to use—just flip the cap closed and make sure it seals—and you don't need to purchase separate caps at all. However, their flexible gaskets stiffen with age and need to be replaced every 10 or 20 batches; otherwise, the bottle will lose its ability to hold a seal and fail to carbonate properly. Neither bottle type is innately better or worse than the other, so it's really up to personal preference.

Recycle amber glass beer bottles by sanitizing them and using them for your home brew.

Bottle Capper

This aptly named machine caps your bottles after you've filled them with uncarbonated beer. You can purchase either handheld or bench varieties, but keep in mind that bench bottle cappers are twice as expensive as handheld ones on average, and they use the same principles to work. The major benefit of a bench capper is that your bottle will be held steady as you cap, but unless you have an incredibly

A handheld bottle capper is a cost-effective tool for sealing your bottles of brew.

aggressive capping technique, you should be OK with a handheld one. Handheld bottle cappers come in more expensive electric versions, too.

Bottle Caps

Filled bottles of beer are no good without caps to keep them fresh and let them carbonate. Thankfully, they're quite cheap. You can find them in quantities of 100 or more in a wide variety of colors and designs.

Optional Add-Ons

The rabbit hole of brewing equipment goes much deeper than just the aforementioned essentials. You certainly don't need the following equipment to brew a batch of beer, but these items do make some steps easier or quicker, as well as allow you to customize the flavor and aroma of your beer. After you've brewed a batch or two, consider investing in some of this additional equipment—you're better off waiting until you have more of a feel for the process. If you like the hobby and want to enhance your setup, then the world is your oyster.

Hydrometer

If you want to know the alcohol by volume (ABV) of your home brew, you need to invest in a hydrometer, which is a sealed tube that contains a weighted bulb. It determines the specific density of a liquid; taking an original gravity reading before fermentation and a final gravity reading before bottling and then plugging the numbers into a simple formula will produce an ABV reading. According to Jason Smith of Adventures in Homebrewing (www.homebrewing.org), hydrometers can be used to test grain efficiency and to help with future recipe calculations, too. Although not essential to the brewing process, a hydrometer is a smart investment that lets you connect with your beer on another level. Most will run you around $20.

The hydrometer is a simple tool for measuring your beer's alcohol content.

Hydrometer Test Jar

To properly use a hydrometer, you need to float it in a vial of the liquid you're testing. You can use a pint glass for this, but you're better off just spending the extra few bucks and purchasing a hydrometer test jar that is properly sized for gravity measurement. This way, you won't wind up wasting a full beer to take a hydrometer reading (once you remove the sample, adding it back into the wort is just asking for full-batch contamination). A test jar is basically just a graduated cylinder sized for a hydrometer, and it'll run you less than $5.

Wine Thief

To take a hydrometer reading, you'll need some way to remove a sample of the wort or beer with only minimal disturbance of the yeast and hop sediment, and a wine thief is perfect for that—it works on the

A wine thief simplifies taking a sample of your wort or beer.

same plunger principle as a bottling wand. When you press the release valve at the bottom of the tube, wort flows into the collection tube. Release the valve, and the plunger falls back into place, leaving you with a tube full of wort.

A wine thief will run you between $5 and $10, and I highly recommend one if you'll be using a hydrometer. You can also purchase a wine thief that has been customized to work as a hydrometer test jar, too, allowing you to take your gravity reading and then place the sample back into the wort (do this with caution, however—if that sample is contaminated in any way, you can potentially ruin your entire batch by replacing it).

Hop Bags

If you'll be using whole hops instead of hop pellets in your home brew, do yourself a favor and pick up hop bags before you brew. These mesh bags make adding and removing hop flowers a breeze, significantly lowering the amount of straining and/or skimming you'll need to do. The same goes for steeping grains; in fact, just treat the hops like you would the grains: place them inside the bag, close the drawstring, and let them boil away until flame out. Hop bags come in inexpensive disposable muslin varieties as well as slightly more expensive reusable nylon types.

Wort Chiller

Wort chillers are wonderful pieces of equipment. They use cold water to indirectly cool your wort in a mere fraction of the time that the ice-bath method requires. (For more on the workings of wort chillers, check out page 100 of the Batch Diary, where I talk about using an immersion chiller for the first time.) You can get lower-end immersion models that you hook up to your kitchen (or bathroom) faucet and dunk into your hot wort, while higher-end (such as stainless steel) varieties are more expensive. Counterflow chillers, which run hot wort through copper tubing that is surrounded by a larger-diameter tube through which cold water flows through in the

An immersion chiller hooks up to a faucet and sits in the wort to cool it via cold water running through its copper tubing.

The ice-bath method is the economical way to chill your wort, but tools are available to speed up the process.

opposite direction, cost two or three times as much as the immersion chillers; don't expect to spend less than $200 on one. The ice-bath method may take a lot of time, but it costs next to nothing.

Immersion chillers are easy to use, although they can be difficult to clean if you let them sit after use; rinse them immediately and rinse them well. They take slightly longer to cool than the counterflow varieties, and they also use more water (although arguably still less than an ice bath). Counterflow chillers are the cream of the wort-chiller crop, cooling wort to pitching temperatures in a matter of seconds, but they are more difficult to use, involve multiple parts, and require extensive sanitization. As a novice, you're best served by using an immersion chiller at first, if you decide to use a chiller at all.

Strainer

If you're using whole hops, or if you'd just like to have less sediment in your final product, consider purchasing a strainer to run the wort through before fermenting it. Straining your wort is disputed among home brewers. Some people don't feel that the extra step (and extra piece of equipment/extra chance of contamination) is worth it for just the small amount of additional wort you get at the end, whereas others take more of the waste not, want not approach, straining every last drop of wort out of the brew kettle.

You can also strain your beer between primary and secondary fermentation to remove inactive yeast cells, which helps avoid off-flavors in your final product; in fact, if you'll be doing a secondary fermentation, straining is recommended. If you do decide to strain, make sure that you get a heavy-duty strainer, preferably stainless steel for its strength and stain-free properties. You don't need a large model; a 10-inch diameter should suffice.

Bottling Tree

This is another piece of optional equipment that I strongly recommend. Basically just a plastic stand with hooks for bottles, a bottling tree will help give you peace of mind as you clean and sanitize your bottles on bottling day. The hooks are usually set at 45-degree angles, which will allow the bottles to drain and dry before being filled with delicious home brew, and the angled design also helps keep dust particles and pet dander from settling in the bottles as they sit. These are a bit pricey, so expect to spend up to $30 for a 45-bottle tree and up to $60 for larger models. The smaller models are definitely worth the expense, though.

A bottling tree helps keep your sanitized bottles clean while they are drying.

Kegging Setup

Kegging your beer simplifies the beer storage process and saves significant time over bottling, but it will require a modest monetary outlay for even the most basic system. Perhaps the greatest advantage of kegging is that your beer can be carbonated and ready to serve within two to three days compared to the several weeks that bottle conditioning requires. For an entry-level kegging setup, expect to spend a few hundred dollars plus significantly more for the advanced systems required to store and dispense your beer. I strongly recommend that you bottle the first couple of batches before making the switch to kegging; while bottling does take more time, it helps you learn the basics before making a serious investment in equipment.

Equipment Kits

As the name suggests, these kits contain all the physical tools you'll need to brew, ferment, and bottle a batch of beer. They will vary slightly from manufacturer to manufacturer, both in price and included items, but even the most basic kits provide the majority of what you'll need, including a fermentor (either a plastic or glass carboy or a plastic bottling bucket; a deluxe kit will likely contain both), an airlock, sanitizer and/or cleanser, a thermometer, a racking cane and tubing, a bottling wand, a bottle brush, and a bottle capper. A more advanced kit might include a brew pot, an instructional DVD, a bottle tree, a hydrometer, bottle caps, and a wort chiller.

Equipment kits run the pricing gamut, ranging from $50 for a bare-bones kit up to more than $300 for a high-end, deluxe collection. Expect to spend around $100 to get basic supplies that are of good enough quality to last through potentially dozens of batches.

Where to Buy

As home brewing continues to grow in popularity, the availability of supplies is (pleasantly) increasing. You can find both equipment and equipment kits at a variety of locations, including beer bars, larger liquor stores, and specialty home-brewing supply stores, if you're lucky. To find your nearest retailer, visit the American Homebrewers Association website (www.homebrewersassociation.org), click on "Let's Brew" and then "Find a Homebrew Supply Shop" and input your state to find a comprehensive list of licensed distributors near you.

Even if you don't live near a supply store, the Internet has you covered. (Check out the Resources in the back of the book for a list of some online brewing suppliers.) If you do order online, I'd caution you away from reading too many reviews—it's far too easy to get sucked into a spiral of negative reviews from grumpy home brewers. Just find a decently rated piece of equipment and take the plunge; odds are, you'll be fine. You can always upgrade to a more expensive version later.

Take It Slow

Don't let the equipment costs and types daunt you. Everything you'll be using to brew your first batch is easy to understand, and you can invest in some of the optional pieces as you continue to pursue the hobby.

Brewing Steps

We've covered beer's lengthy history, we've delved deep into the required home-brewing ingredients, and we've covered the finer points of a basic equipment setup. Now, finally, we're ready to cover the most important part of the home-brewing process: brew day! This is the afternoon or evening when you'll start with those four basic ingredients and finish with a fermentor full of wort, just waiting to become delicious, eminently sippable beer.

It may seem overwhelming now, but beer is a relatively easy beverage to create. The hardest part about brewing is waiting for the beer to ferment and carbonate! I've broken down the brewing process into easily digestible steps, and you'll use this same basic structure for your first batch of beer and every batch after. When you prepare to make your own first batch of home brew, follow a tested recipe, such as one of those in the Chapter 14, Beer Recipes, and keep this chapter bookmarked (as well as the Batch Diary, Chapter 8) so you'll know what to expect as you brew.

One last thing before I break it all down: we have to discuss the most important facet of home brewing. It's not nearly as exciting as adding hops and pitching yeast, but it is basically the lifeblood of your home brew and what keeps your beer safe and delicious: cleaning and sanitizing your equipment.

Sanitize, Sanitize, Sanitize

It doesn't matter how perfect your recipe ratios are or what inventive style you'll be trying: if you don't brew with clean, sanitized equipment, you're shooting yourself in the foot before you even begin. Without a proper regimen of first cleaning and then sanitizing, you risk jeopardizing the entire batch of beer to a host of wild yeasts and bacteria that can produce off-flavors and render your home brew completely undrinkable, not to mention wasting your time and money.

Although not the most exciting of subjects, cleaning and sanitizing are vital for ensuring the success of every brewing endeavor. When I talk about cleaning throughout this chapter (and the book), I'm referring specifically to the physical removal of debris and grime, while sanitizing refers to the reduction of microorganisms on equipment and bottles through chemical or other means. (Don't confuse sanitizing with sterilizing—sterilizing is basically an impossibility at home. You're just looking to minimize the amount of microorganisms as much as possible.)

Cleaner Options

The first and last step in the brewing process is cleaning. With elbow grease and a cleaning agent, a brewer can efficiently remove from the equipment any residues, stains, and physical debris that provide a home to unwanted microorganisms. Home brewers use several agents to help with the cleaning process: mild detergents, bleach solutions, and sodium percarbonate.

Many home brewers tend to gravitate toward the sodium percarbonate family of cleaners, which include Oxi-Clean, Arm and Hammer Super Washing Soda, One Step, and Powdered Brewery Wash. Unlike bleach and detergents, sodium percarbonate can be used on all materials and does not leave residues that harm the quality of your beer. (Lack of residue is the biggest reason to opt for the percarbonate cleaners—you do not want to taste soap when you should be tasting malt and hops.) When mixed with water, sodium percarbonate powders create an oxidizing effect that breaks down dirt and can clean every item needed to brew beer. They are relatively safe, environmentally friendly, effective, and especially good at cleaning hard-to-reach areas, like the interior of tubing. Your local home-brew supply store likely carries a number of varieties. Different percarbonate cleaners have slightly different formulations and contact times, and some require rinsing, so make sure you fully read the label of your chosen cleaner before you put it into use.

I've used both Oxi-Clean and Powdered Brewery Wash in the past, and I liked both of them. I default to Oxi-Clean these days because I can also use it elsewhere around the house, and my local grocery store always carries it, but you can't really go wrong with any of these percarbonate options—read the labels and pick which one works best for you.

Numerous sanitizing solutions are available to the home brewer.

The dishwasher is an effective sanitizer for glass bottles.

Sanitizer Options

Only after your equipment has been well cleaned can you achieve proper sanitization. There are several commercial sanitizing products specifically for home brewing, including iodine- and acid-based sanitizers. Iodine-based sanitizers, like IO Star and BTF Iodophor, usually don't require rinsing and have a very short contact time. A downside to iodine sanitizers is that they tend to stain plastic equipment, and they lose efficacy quickly once mixed with water. Acid-based sanitizers, such as Star San and Saniclean, are also no-rinse sanitizers with a low contact time. When used in solution, acid-based sanitizers create a harmless foam, do not stain, and can be stored for long periods after mixing.

You can also use a solution of unscented bleach—one tablespoon per gallon of water—as an effective sanitizer. The downside is that equipment sanitized with bleach must be thoroughly—and I mean thoroughly—rinsed with hot water to avoid imparting off-flavors to the beer.

Dishwashers remain one of the few nonchemical options available to home brewers. The steam created by the dishwasher's drying cycle can effectively sanitize your equipment, but it is not recommended for plastic items, which can be damaged by excess heat.

Personally, I prefer iodine-based sanitizers when I brew. They're cheaper than their acid-based counterparts, I've not had any issues with permanent equipment stains, the required contact time for proper sanitization is manageable, and I've never had any spoiled batches (so far). For your first batch, I'd recommend going with either an iodine- or acid-based option because bleach and dishwashers are a little less reliable, and you definitely want your initial brew to succeed.

No matter which option you choose, it is essential that you read and closely follow the guidelines for that sanitizing agent. If your sanitizing solutions are too diluted, they will not work effectively; if they are too strong, they waste costly sanitizer and can even negatively affect your beer. I cannot overemphasize the importance of learning about your specific agents and how to properly apply them. To consistently brew successful beers, batch after batch, you need to develop thorough and efficient cleaning and sanitizing habits. These habits start with knowing how to correctly use all of your cleaning and sanitizing products.

Brew Day Prep and Cleanup

When preparing for the big brewing day, you need to think through the cleaning and sanitizing steps. Any utensils that touch the wort after the boil will need to be thoroughly sanitized. This includes stainless-steel spoons, funnels, all tubing, the siphon equipment, the carboy or fermenting bucket, the stopper/lid, the blow-off hose, and any sampling tools. Because it will contain the boiling wort, the brew pot does not need to be cleaned before you begin. Also think about keeping a small container of no-rinse sanitizer or a sanitized tray on which to rest any utensils used more than once.

Get Started

Now that you understand how important clean, sanitized equipment is to home brewing, let's dive in for real. A note before we get started: there are two optional steps that are required for all-grain brewing. I include them in case any of you home-brewing novices are feeling particularly adventurous and also because going all-grain is a natural next step in the evolution of your home-brewing process. These steps are marked as all grain steps, so if you're brewing with extract, be it wet or dry, you won't need to worry about grinding your grain or lautering and sparging your wort.

Step 1: Grind Your Grain
(Optional—All-Grain)

The first step in brewing beer is to grind the grain that will go into your mash, says Erik Nielsen, co-owner of Two Shy Brewing in Roseburg, Oregon. "If you just put the grain in water, it's not going to do anything," he notes, "so you need to crack the grains, which exposes the inner starches and lets the enzyme get to the core so it can extract them and convert them to sugar."

The tool of choice: a manual or motorized roller mill grinder that pulls the husks off the grains while keeping them intact. An old sausage grinder is an effective and economical choice for home brewers, but it can pulverize the entire kernel, husk and all, and that could create problems in the brewing process.

Grinding your grain is the first step in all-grain brewing.

"Those husks create a natural filter that helps prevent the sparge from getting stuck," Nielsen adds. "If you use a sausage grinder, you can add an alternative hull, like rice hulls, to get that same filtration. It just won't be part of the barley."

Extract note: If you're brewing from extract, the steeping grains you purchased (or that came in your recipe kit) will already be cracked, so this step will already be done for you. If you crack the grains yourself on brew day, you'll get fresher flavor from the barley.

Step 2: Make the Mash

Heat up the water in your brew kettle or hot liquor tank (HLT). It needs to be brought up to temperature to activate the enzymes and start the mash's starch-to-sugar conversion process.

"Depending on the style of beer you're making, the optimal temperature for mashing is 148 to 170 degrees [Fahrenheit]," Nielsen notes. "We want to hit 152 to 158, but it can go all the way down to 148 or 145. If you go over 170, you kill it; if you go too low, it doesn't do anything."

When the water's ready, add the grain and let it soak for as long as your recipe dictates—this can range between 20 minutes and a full hour. "Keep it in a container that can maintain temperature," Nielsen says. "Some people put it in a pot on a stove and keep heat under it to maintain it. Other people will put it in an insulated cooler that's been converted into a mash tub, which works very well for home brewers."

For your first batch, your brew kettle will work just fine. Try to maintain the recipe-recommended temperature as much as you can, and make sure that you don't exceed 170 degrees F if at all possible. Staying within the optimal temperature range will pull out the colors and flavors from your steeping grains and give the best possible end result. If you're using just a brew kettle, you'll want to place your grains in a mesh steeping bag for easy removal; this will also allow you to skip Step 3.

Step 3: Lauter and Sparge
(Optional—All-Grain)

Once the grain has soaked and the starches have converted to sugar, it's time to separate the wort, or sugar water, from the grain via filtering and sparging—a process called *lautering*.

The tool for this step is a lauter tun, which is a large vessel that holds the mash. It has either a false bottom or a manifold to allow the wort to drain out while leaving the grain behind, Nielsen explains. "You'll drain the sugar water off, and then you rinse, or sparge, the grain," he says. "You want to do it to stop the conversion process and rinse off whatever sugars are still in the grain and push that into your boil kettle."

You can *batch-sparge*, which means draining the wort completely from the mash and then adding more 170-degree water and draining again, or *fly sparge* (a continuous sparge), where you add water at the same slow rate at which the wort is drained.

"Then, it all goes into the kettle and homogenizes," Nielsen says. "The mash will be super syrupy and full of sugar, and the sparge will be a lot more diluted."

Extract note: These steps are optional. If you're brewing with extracts, you don't have the required equipment, or you'd rather just not hassle with lautering, you can simply remove the mesh bag that contains your steeping grains and let the liquid drain as much as possible without squeezing the bag. From here, you can proceed to Step 4.

Lautering separates the spent grain from the liquid.

Step 4: Boil the Wort

The next step is to boil the wort and add your bittering, flavoring, and finishing hops. "The fun part is deciding how long of a boil you're going to do," Nielsen says. "The minimum time is 20 minutes, and the traditional boil is 60 minutes, but you could let it go for 90 minutes. The longer you boil, the more caramel flavor you're going to get."

The hops can be added before the boil or at any time during the boil. Bittering hops are typically boiled for 45 to 90 minutes, flavoring hops are boiled for 20 to 40 minutes, and finishing hops are added during the final minutes of the boil. Bittering hops are added first because the longer the hops boil, the more bitter they become, so this first addition helps balance out the wort's innate sweetness. Flavoring hops are added in the back third of the boil, where they can impart flavor—aptly named, no?—to the wort, while aroma (finishing) hops are added right at the end so you can smell them when you first pour your beer.

"The flavoring and finishing additions are going to give you the aroma of the flower or the variety of hop that you choose," Nielsen said. "There are all sorts of variations on this, which is what makes each recipe unique."

Your individual recipe will dictate how long the boil should last and how to time the addition of your hops. As Nielsen says, deciding on these hop additions is one of the fun parts of home brewing and recipe development, but for your initial batch, color inside the recipe lines, so to speak.

The traditional boil typically lasts for a total of 60 minutes, with hops added at intervals throughout.

Step 5: Flame Out

After you've boiled, bittered, and flavored the wort, you'll cut the flame. You will then chill the mixture as quickly as possible in an ice-water bath or with a plate chiller or an immersion chiller, Nielsen suggests. "You're trying to bring that wort temperature down to 70 or 80 degrees [Fahrenheit] as quickly as possible to yeast-pitchable temperature," he says. "This is the stage where you are the most vulnerable. Any bacteria that falls in there won't die because it's not hot enough, so everything at that point has to be sanitary. Even the spoon has to be sterile before you use it."

Once the wort has cooled to room temperature, it's time for the fermentor.

Once the wort hits room temperature, transfer it to your fermentor. Strain out the hops and other proteins with a stainless-steel strainer or carefully decant the wort, leaving the material behind. Whirlpooling is an option, too, Nielsen says. "Whirlpooling gathers the hops into the center of the pot," he adds. "It enables you to siphon off clear wort from the side."

This is a good opportunity to take a sample of the wort so you can measure its gravity, Nielsen recommends. "It's your starting point," he says, "which you're going to need to calculate how much alcohol you're going to potentially have versus how much you actually get."

Because this is your first batch, the ice-bath method is probably your best bet because it's the slowest of the chilling methods as well as the cheapest and the one that doesn't require any additional equipment. Basically, you want to set your covered brew kettle in a bathtub or kitchen sink that you've filled with ice water and allow the cold water to bring the boiling wort back down into the room-temperature range. Unfortunately, this can take upward of half an hour, so make sure that you keep the kettle covered (even though the temptation is to let the steam escape for a quicker cool). Check the temperature only occasionally because lifting the lid risks contamination.

Eventually, you'll probably want to invest in a wort chiller, which will speed up the process considerably. There are different types of wort chillers, but it's not required equipment, especially when you are just starting out.

Step 6: Let It Bubble

The final step of brew day is to add (pitch), your yeast to start the fermentation process. Put on the lid, seal it, and rock the vessel back and forth to evenly distribute the yeast. Place the sanitized airlock and stopper in place, put the fermentor in a protected area with a stable temperature—usually between 65–75 degrees F, although your yeast strain and your recipe will dictate this exact temperature range—and let the yeast go to work, Nielsen says. "Just let it ferment," he advises, noting that activity should start within 12 to 24 hours. Three days at 65–70 degrees F is the typical fermenting time for a pale ale.

At this point, you need to decide whether you're going to use a single- or two stage fermentation process for your beer. You can either leave it in the fermentor for two to three weeks while the beer conditions, or you can move it to a second vessel through a process called *racking*.

Racking is when you transfer the beer to a second fermentor without disturbing the sediments or exposing it to air. The process is typically done by siphoning. "You will have about a 1-inch layer of sediment at the bottom of the carboy," Nielsen says. "That sediment is going to be any hop particulates that got transferred over from the boil, natural proteins that have developed in the beer, and any dead yeast particles. When you rack the beer, you're trying to remove the beer off that layer of sediment."

Some beer styles require a secondary fermentation for additional flavor and clarity, but for your first batch of home brew, a primary fermentation will do just fine.

Step 7: Clean Up

After the boil, your brew pot will be a sticky mess. You should clean it as soon as you finish pitching your yeast and moving your fermentor to its temporary location. Fill the brew pot with warm water, soak it for an hour, and then use a pot scrubber approved for stainless steel to remove any crud or burnt spots. Do not use bleach or stainless-steel scouring pads; these

You know that your brew is fermenting when you see bubbles in the airlock.

methods can damage and even rust the vessel. For extra-tough stains, use an over-the-counter cleaner approved for stainless steel, such as Bar Keepers Friend. Rinse the pot really well when you are finished, especially if you use cleaning agents. Do not forget to soak, clean, and sanitize the remaining equipment as soon as possible before storage.

Step 8: Priming and Bottling

Whether you decide to use a single- or two-stage fermentation process, you can expect to prime and bottle your beer in two to three weeks, or when fermentation is complete. This isn't actually a brew-day step, and there's even an entire chapter about priming and bottling (see Chapter 6), but, for now, you only need to know that priming is when you add sugar water to the batch of beer just before bottling it. The sugar gives the yeast one more little boost of activity, and that naturally creates your beer's carbonation.

"That yeast is still in suspension," Nielsen says, "so when we bottle, we'll clean the bottles, boil a cup and a half of sugar water on the stove, dilute it, chill it down, quickly add it to the wort that's at room temperature, stir it up real quick, and add just one more little boost of sugar for those guys to eat."

He continues: "Then you bottle it and cap it, [and then] you store it again at room temperature for about a week, and the yeast that was still in suspension will continue to feed on that sugar water you just put in."

When you're ready to bottle, make sure that you use cleaned and sanitized bottles and caps that you've scrubbed with a nylon bottle brush and soaked in sanitizing solution. You also can sanitize them in a bleach solution and rinse well.

Bottling and capping take place several weeks after brew day.

After your beer has been primed, slowly fill the bottles. Use a fill tube and take care to prevent gurgling and aeration. Fill to about three-quarters of an inch from the top of the bottle and then cap.

Step 9: Enjoy! (Eventually)

The final step in home brewing is waiting: those beers need a few weeks to bottle-condition and carbonate properly. When it's finally time to crack open a cold one and taste your hard work, pour the beer slowly into a glass to avoid disturbing the yeast layer on the bottom. Drink with a clean, neutral palate, if possible, and try to taste the flavors of the hops, the grain, and the malt in your recipe. Most importantly: sit back, relax, and enjoy the fruits of your labor!

But let's not get ahead of ourselves here. You've brewed successfully, and your very first batch of beer is bubbling away in the closet. Let's take a look at those priming and bottling steps a little more closely in the next chapter.

6

Bottling Steps

After brew day, a new beer is (hopefully) bubbling away in your carboy or fermenting bucket. Now is the time to consider the future home for your freshly brewed beverage. Although a broad range of individual options exist, they boil down to two general categories: bottling and kegging. The most common choice for new and intermediate home brewers is bottling due to the low startup costs and simple equipment required. For more advanced home brewers who produce several batches per month, kegging can be a useful time-saving option.

For the purposes of your first batch, bottling is strongly recommended. Once you progress to the advanced stages of home brewing, or you begin brewing more frequently, the investment in kegging equipment may be worth your time, but when you're just getting your feet wet, kegging is unnecessary; your bottle-conditioned beer will be just as delicious as a force-carbonated, kegged home brew.

A hydrometer reading can tell you if your beer is ready for bottling.

When Is the Beer Ready to Bottle?

First, you'll need to figure out if your beer is ready to be bottled. Each beer recipe is slightly different, but most home-brewed ales finish their primary fermentation and begin to clarify after seven to fourteen days in the fermentor. To ensure that your beer is ready to bottle, take one last hydrometer reading to check the final gravity and see that it matches the target gravity range specified in the recipe.

Make sure that your sampling tools are sanitized before taking the sample, and do not return the sample to the fermentor. (I know you're tired of hearing about sanitization, but it's absolutely essential!) The temperature of your beer can impact your hydrometer reading, so don't forget to factor in the temperature of the sample using the conversion chart that comes with most hydrometers.

If you're not using a hydrometer, or if you'd rather not take any measurements, you can judge by the bubbles in the airlock: if you haven't seen any activity in 48 hours, your beer has completed primary fermentation. The hydrometer is more accurate, of course, so consider eventually purchasing one to test the end of primary fermentation—just remember that continuous readings will leave you with less of your final product, and you risk contamination with every sample.

Is your beer ready to bottle, but you're too busy to do it? Just leave the beer in your carboy or fermenting bucket. Some additional time in a dark fermentor will not harm your new brew, but just be careful that you don't leave it for too long. A week is usually OK, but any longer than that can start to produce some off-flavors (see Chapter 11, Troubleshooting).

Selecting Your Bottles

The first item on your agenda is to get your bottles together while the beer continues to ferment. You can choose from several types of bottles: 12-ounce longneck bottles, 22-ounce bomber bottles, and 16- or

32-ounce swing-top bottles with ceramic stoppers and gaskets. Be sure to use only amber-colored bottles because, as mentioned earlier, clear or green glass bottles allow too much light to reach your beer, which will degrade it and cause a skunky flavor, writes Sam Calagione, founder and president of Dogfish Head Craft Brewery, in *Extreme Brewing: An Introduction to Brewing Craft Beer at Home* (Quarry Books).

To bottle a typical 5-gallon batch of home brew, you need to gather fifty longneck bottles, twenty-four to twenty-six bomber bottles, or sixteen to eighteen 32-ounce bottles. Purchasing new bottles from your local home-brew supply store is the safest route, but many folks (myself included) go the green route and recycle commercial beer bottles. When using recycled bottles, make sure that they have traditional American crown caps, not screw tops, which do not seal efficiently. The best policy when recycling bottles is to thoroughly rinse the bottle inside and out with warm water immediately after you finish drinking it—*thoroughly* being the key word. If beer residue dries in the bottom of the bottles, the bottles become extremely difficult to clean and can even become unusable.

If you are using recycled bottles, you'll also want to remove any labels before sanitization. You can do this piecemeal as you collect your bottles, or you can just peel a batch of them on bottling day or the day before—the latter option is my preferred method. The most effective way to get those stubborn labels off is to soak a batch of bottles in a bucket or bathtub filled with hot water for an hour or two. Next, peel off the paper labels and use a scrubbing pad to remove glue residue. For tougher paper labels, consider soaking the bottles in a solution of percarbonate cleaner. After removing the labels, rinse the bottles well, and they'll be ready for sanitizing.

Whether purchased or recycled, you must sanitize all bottles before bottling. A no-rinse sanitizer is easiest: submerge the clean bottles, let them sit for a minute or two, and then empty them and leave them to dry on a sanitized bottling tree. If you are sanitizing swing-top bottles, first remove the gaskets and clean and sanitize the gaskets the same way you sanitize the rest of your equipment.

No matter which style you use, choose amber bottles to best protect your brew from degradation.

If you're not using a bottling tree, your best bet is to leave the bottles submerged until you're ready to use each one—empty a bottle one at a time, fill it according to the following instructions, and go from there. If you pull all of the bottles out and allow them to dry open to the air, then dust, pet dander, and bacteria can settle in the bottles, potentially contaminating them. Better safe than sorry!

You can also save time by sanitizing bottles in your dishwasher. Just place the clean bottles upside down in the dishwasher and run a load with the heated dry (or "sanitize" setting, if available) on without detergent. The resulting heat does an efficient job of sanitizing the bottles. You should use the bottles as soon after sanitizing as possible.

Bottling-Day Prep and Steps

On bottling day, the first step is to gather your equipment: a bottling bucket with a spigot, a racking cane with an auto-siphon, a bottling wand, food-grade tubing that fits your racking cane and wand, and a bottle capper if necessary. Make sure to sanitize all of this equipment except the capper because it won't be coming into contact with anything that will also directly be touching the beer.

Don't forget to sanitize the individual parts of the spigot assembly on the bottle bucket as well as the bottle caps. Soak traditional unlined metal bottle caps in sanitizing solution or boil them for 15 minutes—soaking them gives you the best peace of mind. If you're using high-end caps with oxygen-absorbing liners, sanitize them only with iodine or acid-based sanitizers, such as Iodophor or Star San, or else the liner will be rendered useless—no bleach here!

Priming and Racking Your Beer

Beer directly out of the fermentor is flat and needs to be primed to gradually carbonate in the bottle. As previously mentioned, its flavor is all there—and if you're taking a final gravity reading with a hydrometer, you should taste your sample to get an idea of how your final product will taste—but it just doesn't have those effervescent bubbles yet.

The simplest way to add bubbles to your beer is by adding a sugar solution, which reactivates the remaining live yeast cells and results in carbonation. This final fermentation takes place in a sealed container, so the carbon dioxide produced by the yeast has nowhere to go, resulting in a carbonated end

A bottle tree keeps those sanitized bottles clean while they are waiting to be filled.

product. Follow your beer recipe and use the exact type of sugar and the correct proportion of water to sugar. Different sugar types can carbonate at different levels and add slightly different flavors to your beer (see "Priming Sugar Types" on page 64).

To make your priming solution, which is just a simple syrup, bring the water to a boil in a saucepan, add the sugar, let it dissolve, and allow the mixture to return to a boil. Remove the saucepan from the heat, cover it with a sanitized lid, and let the priming solution cool. Once it is cooled, pour the liquid into the bottom of your bottling bucket unless the recipe states otherwise. Some recipes will advise you to add the priming sugar on top of the beer and stir with a sanitized spoon. If your recipe doesn't specify when to add the sugar, feel free to add it first, which will save you the stirring step.

Making a sugar solution helps distribute the sugar evenly throughout the beer.

Move your fermentor to a countertop or table, taking care not to disturb the sediment deposits in the base. Place the bottling bucket on the floor or on a stable chair directly below the fermentor—this height difference helps harness the power of gravity, which is essential for proper siphoning. Remove the airlock and stopper or top from the fermentor and place your racking cane into the fermentor just above the sediment in the base. If your racking cane comes with a clip (and most do), clip the cane to the side of your fermentor to hold it in place.

Start the siphon and begin transferring the beer into the bottling bucket, keeping the receiving end of the tubing in the bucket below the surface of the priming liquid. Slowly transfer the beer, trying not to splash, because splashing will aerate the beer and introduce unwanted oxygen. Stop the siphon when there is about an inch of liquid left. You'll be leaving a little beer behind, but that beer also contains significant portions of hop residue and dead yeast cells that you don't necessarily want to be drinking.

Filling Your Bottles

Once the transfer is complete, carefully relocate your bottling bucket to the countertop or tabletop and move your fermentor out of the way. Attach one end of the tubing to the bucket's spigot and your bottling wand to the far end of the tubing. Make sure that your tubing covers the spigot completely—you don't want any leaks now, in the final steps of the process!

Arrange your sanitized bottles beneath the bottling bucket so that they are within reach of the bottling wand. (This is where a bottling tree comes in handy—you can just move it, and thus all of your bottles, in one go.) Open the spigot and press the spring-loaded tip of the bottling wand into the bottom of a bottle, allowing the beer to slowly fill the bottle. Fill to near the top of the bottle and then withdraw the wand. You create the necessary headspace in the bottle by removing the wand. Either cap each bottle with a sanitized cap or close the bottle's swing top.

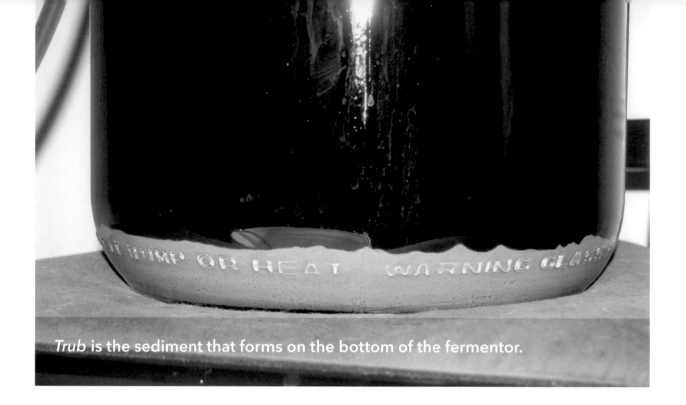

Trub is the sediment that forms on the bottom of the fermentor.

The bottling process is easier with two people—one to fill and one to cap—especially if you are filling fifty bottles. The person taking on the capping duties will also be able to tip the bottling bucket toward the spigot to get those last drops of liquid at the end of the process. If you're flying solo with 12-ounce bottles or bombers, you can fill a bottle and then just place an unfastened cap on top of the neck to save time and protect your beer—after you've filled all the bottles, go through with your capper and seal the caps.

After all of your bottles are capped, wipe them down and store them in a dark place, like a closet or basement, at room temperature. Although amber-colored bottles will protect your beer from the ultraviolet rays that can cause skunky flavors, it's best not to take any chances, especially if you're using clear swing-top bottles.

Last But Not Least

The last thing you want to do after filling and capping your last bottle is tackle the mountain of dirty equipment—I hear that. However reluctant you may feel, though, it is essential that you move quickly, because if left dirty, the tubing and other small components you just used can become impossible to clean, degrading their performance and potentially losing their ability to be thoroughly sanitized for the next batch. Pop open a beer to help soften the blow (not one of the ones you just bottled, of course!), and let's get cleaning.

First, rinse your tubing, racking cane, carboy stopper, airlock, and bottling wand. Take apart any items than can

With a racking cane and siphon, transfer the liquid into the bottling bucket.

Priming Sugar Types

Although table and corn sugar are probably the most common priming sugars used in home brewing, they're not the only varieties that can be used. As long as you're adding some kind of sugar to your beers before you bottle-condition them, you'll have a carbonated final product. Here are some of the more common types of sugars used in home brewing.

Table or corn sugar: The flavorlessness and easy accessibility of these sugars make them the most common option for priming sugars. They're dependable, they easily dissolve into a simple syrup, and you've likely already got some in your kitchen cabinets. However, don't use powdered or icing sugar as a priming agent because small amounts of cornstarch are added to prevent clumping, and you don't want that in your beer.

Brown or demerara sugar: Used similarly to table sugar, the richness of these sugars can add a deeper note to ales, though they're not recommended for use in a lager.

Honey: Honey can bring a rounder sweetness to ales and lagers and can even bring in additional flavors if you use honey from specific blossoms, such as orange-blossom honey or wildflower honey. If you're making a honey ale or lager, try priming with honey, too, to strengthen those honey notes in the beer.

Syrups: You can use pure maple syrup, molasses, or even sorghum syrup as a priming agent for beers that would benefit from the strong flavor. Maple and sorghum syrups would be nice in an amber ale, while molasses could enrich a stout or porter.

Malt extract: If you'd like to brew an all-malt beer, you can even prime with malt extract, but it's not as predictable and dependable as some of the other options.

When you're first starting out, you'll be best served by using either table or corn sugar because they won't have any impact on the final product's taste. However, as you progress with your home brews, consider swapping them out for some of the more flavorful options. The priming sugar taste differences aren't pervasive, but they can round out and deepen the flavors already present in your home brew.

Whichever priming sugar you use, crunch the numbers first to make sure that you add the right amount—too much, and your bottles can explode; too little will produce an undercarbonated beer, which is only one step up from a flat beer in terms of drinkability.

Use the power of gravity to help you fill your bottles.

be taken apart and then place this equipment in a solution of percarbonate cleaner (or the cleaner of your choice) and let it sit for 15 to 20 minutes; a rinsed bottling bucket (with the spigot closed) is great for this.

While those pieces soak, start working on your carboy or fermenting bucket. Give it an initial scrub with a large nylon bottle brush or angled carboy brush and then fill it with a cleaning solution—I recommend percarbonate, but whatever you choose will work (just avoid soap because its residues can negatively affect the next batch of beer; see Chapter 11, Troubleshooting). Letting the fermentor soak for a couple of hours or overnight will loosen the caked-on sediment and foam, but you should be able to get most, if not all, of your sediment off after a brief soak. Partially drain the fermentor and then use elbow grease and a brush to remove any stains or sediment. Rinse thoroughly and let the fermentor dry completely before storing it.

Return to the items in the bottling bucket while the fermentor soaks. Run the cleaning solution through the tubing using the racking cane and bottling wand to make sure that every nook and cranny is fully exposed. Use your small nylon bottle and tube brushes to remove visible gunk, then rinse with more cleaner. Once cleaned, let the equipment air-dry and then stow it in a clean bin for your next batch.

The Waiting Game

After your beer is safely bottled, it will need one to three weeks to become fully carbonated and to clarify—this process is called *bottle conditioning*. To check if carbonation is occurring, hold a bottle up to the light: if you see sediment accumulating in the bottom, it suggests that the carbonation process is under way. To confirm, chill a single bottle and then crack it open and enjoy.

If low carbonation is an issue, just keep conditioning for an additional week or two. This is

How to Use a Siphon

Siphons, specifically the hose and racking cane variety, can be a little confusing to start if you're not sure exactly how they work. (If you splurged on an auto-siphon, congratulations–you can skip this sidebar entirely.) The first time I home brewed, we couldn't get the siphon started properly, so my friend Dustin had to suck on the end of the hose to make it work. Our beer wasn't contaminated, thankfully (and luckily), but sucking on the siphon tubing with your bacteria-ridden mouth is not recommended, no matter how much vodka or mouthwash you gargle in your sanitizing attempts.

The proper way to start a siphon is to first sanitize the entire thing: tubing, racking cane, etc. Next, fill the tubing with liquid–preferably sanitizer, but you can also use water, if you'd like. Now drain that sanitizer into a separate container, which will pull a little beer with it. Once you see the liquid in the container change from the sanitizer to beer, clamp the siphon closed. Move the hose from the separate container to your bottling bucket and open the siphon–voilà!

I like to use the kitchen faucet to start the siphon, and then I siphon sanitizer through the entire tube. Finally, after the sanitizer starts coming out the other end, I'll switch to beer. You can also purchase a siphon starter to make the process a little easier, but once you've used a racking cane once, it will be pretty easy to manage.

especially true if you are brewing a beer with higher alcohol content, which usually requires more time to achieve proper carbonation. Bottle conditioning also helps develop the flavor of a beer. Certain styles, like stouts and porters, particularly benefit from an extra month or two of bottle conditioning to mature their flavors. In general, most home brews should be consumed before six months of age and definitely within a year because oxidation sets in and degrades the beer.

Even though some beers are ready after a week of bottle conditioning, I prefer to wait at least two weeks before trying the first bottle—it's tough to wait, but that extra week almost always pays off. And after those two weeks, you can taste your first finished beer and finally sample the fruits of your labor—congratulations! You've finished your first home brew!

As the beer is siphoned out of the fermentor, the yeast leaves a ring of residue behind.

7

Beer Styles

I t should be clear to you now that beer's seeming simplicity is deceptive: a whole lot more goes into producing a bottle than you might imagine at first. But now that you have a little background on this delicious beverage and its multifaceted, wide-reaching history, it's time to move on to one of the backbones of this book: the beer style compendium.

Before delving into the finer points of what makes an IPA (India pale ale) an IPA, a distinction must first be made between the two major beer genres: ales and lagers. Broadly speaking, just about all types of beers can be divided into these two categories. There are certainly crossovers, hybrids, and obscure varieties, but the real difference between the two essentially comes down to whether the yeast is top-fermented (ales) or bottom-fermented (lagers), which plays a large part in each beer's overall taste and color.

Top-fermented beers—ales—are brewed at warmer temperatures and use yeast that rises to the top during fermentation. Bottom-fermented beers—lagers—are brewed at colder temperatures and use yeast that sinks to the bottom during fermentation.

There's more to it than yeast varieties, though. As mentioned, ales and lagers are fermented at different temperatures, and fermentation temperature plays a huge role in the eventual taste, feel, and color of a beer. Ales are brewed at a temperature of about 65 to 70 degrees F, whereas lagers require colder brewing conditions of about 40 to 55 degrees F.

Due to the temperature difference, ales complete the fermentation process faster than lagers. The warmer brewing conditions of ales allow the yeast to ferment quickly—about a week is common—while the cooler conditions that lagers need cause the yeast to work very slowly, which can require months of fermentation. (The end result is totally worth it, though. You take one sip of your first home-brewed lager, and all of those weeks of waiting just evaporate.)

The cool fermentation temperatures of lagers restrict the growth of some yeast types, which means that ales tend to have richer, stronger flavors, while lagers lean toward the mellower, cleaner, crisper side of the taste spectrum. Either type can be pale or dark, but lagers tend to be paler than ales. Lagers are also best served at colder temperatures, near the freezing point, while ales tend to be best at warmer temperatures—not necessarily room temperature, but 50 degrees F or so will bring out an ale's true flavor profile.

Notes on Styles and Terminology

Rarely are beer styles set in stone, especially in today's craft-beer movement that so dearly prizes creativity. You'll find some brews that adhere to style guidelines very closely and others that taste almost like style blends. One of the most common variations is the hop level and resulting bitterness: American craft brews tend to favor aggressive hopping across the board. These style notes are designed to give you a general outline of the beer types, but when you're designing your own brew recipes, feel free to experiment either within or outside of style parameters discussed throughout this chapter—that's half the fun of home brewing!

I've designed the notes in this chapter to be general guidelines. You're very likely to find an aggressively hopped amber ale or a fruit-forward cream ale on the market somewhere. I briefly discuss the following six points for each beer variety.

Color: Somewhat subjective, beer color can vary wildly between styles due to the grains used in making the wort, the length of the boil, and the hops and flavoring agents used in the brewing process.

Flavor: In the descriptions of the numerous beer styles, I've tried to give you an idea of what flavor notes to expect from each. Although there is considerable variation in each, due to the grains, hops, and flavoring agents used and how the fermenting process changes from brewery to brewery, there will still be some constants across the board.

Alcohol content: Alcohol content is measured in alcohol by volume (ABV). The value refers to what percentage of the final product's volume is alcohol. Low-alcohol beers tend to clock in between 2 and 4 percent, while high-alcohol styles, like barleywines, can be as high as 12 to 14 percent. (Alcoholic beverages can also be measured in proof count, which is simply double the ABV percentage; vodka, for instance, is commonly 40 percent ABV or 80 proof. However, proof count is almost unseen in beers and is usually reserved for spirits.)

Breweries often offer flights, or samplers, of their craft beers.

Bitterness: For each style, I've given a bitterness range measured in international bittering units (IBUs). The lower the range, the less bitter the beer will be: if you're looking for a low-IBU beer, consider an American lager; if you're looking to push the limits of beer's bitterness, an imperial IPA or barleywine is right up your alley. IBU values range from 0 to 120.

Glass: Though it may seem like you can just drink beer out of any old glass—and, let's be honest, you can—beers taste best out of glasses designed to maximize their style's flavors and aromas. You can find detailed descriptions of each later in this chapter.

Examples: For each style, I've included three commercial examples on the market today. The chosen examples are either some of the most common varieties available or excellent exemplars of what a style has to offer—or maybe even brews that push the style's boundaries. Some might be seasonal offerings. For more information on each, check out the specific brewery's website.

One final note: This is not meant to be an exhaustive catalog of the beer styles on the market today. The styles not mentioned here are either obscure in the American market (e.g., the German *gose* or British *braggot*) or are difficult to recreate at home for certain reasons—you won't find lambics or American wild ales in this chapter because they're brewed with wild yeast, which is hard enough to manage in a commercial setting. These descriptions are simply meant to familiarize you with what you'll be able to pick up at your local liquor store or beer distributor and recreate—or riff on—at home. If a style you're looking for isn't listed here, check out www.craftbeer.com/beer-styles or www.beeradvocate.com/beer/style for two of the more comprehensive guides the Internet has to offer.

Ales

Ales encompass a broader taste spectrum than their lager brethren, and because of their comparative ease of brewing, there are a wider number of ale styles. Let's crack open the top of these delicious brews.

The different sizes and shapes of beer glasses lend themselves to particular beer styles.

American Amber Ale

The American amber ale is somewhat of a catchall category: any brews lighter in color are considered pale ales, and darker ones are likely going to be categorized as brown ales or dark ales. The hops levels in these beers can vary dramatically, with some breweries treating them similarly to an IPA while also focusing on the malts that give the brews their signature color.

Color: The color can vary between pale amber to deep red; this category is a sort of catchall, so any ales between pale ales and brown ales would likely fall here.

Flavor: Amber ales are usually quite balanced, with decent hoppiness and a broad malty character. Again, because the style varies so much, it's hard to nail down a specific common flavor, though citrus notes are common, as are caramels from the malty character. Most—although definitely far from all—have relatively mild flavor.

Alcohol content: Between 4 and 7 percent

Bitterness: Between 30 and 45 IBU, on average

Glass: Shaker pint

Examples: Bell's Amber Ale, Bell's Brewery, Inc.; Fat Tire Amber Ale, New Belgium Brewing; Nosferatu, Great Lakes Brewing Company

American Barleywine

Don't be fooled by the name: barleywine is decidedly not wine; rather, it is an incredibly strong and intense style of beer. Barleywines get their name because they can be stored for years and aged like wines, and their alcohol content is usually similar to a wine's. Not for the faint of heart, barleywines have high ABVs and are typically aggressively hopped, resulting in strong herbal, fruity flavors. The hoppiness is somewhat balanced by a malty sweetness, especially in English barleywines, although they're often bittersweet in the end. Barleywines made with at least 50 percent wheat malts are known as wheat wines.

Color: The color can range anywhere from amber to dark brown.

Flavor: Some barleywines are fruit-forward while some are more resiny and herbal, depending on the hop varieties used. Because of the high ABV, most barleywines also have a noticeable alcohol taste.

Alcohol content: Between 8 and 12 percent (some can even be as high as 15 percent!)

Bitterness: Between 60 and 100 IBUs, on average

Glass: Snifter

Examples: Evil Twin Freudian Slip, Evil Twin Brewing; Olde School Barleywine, Dogfish Head Brewery; Old Horizontal, Victory Brewing Company

American Brown Ale

A riff on the English brown ale by early American home brewers, the American brown is another sort of umbrella category: any ale too dark to be an amber ale and too light to be a black ale falls here. Because of this, brown ales can be all over the spectrum in terms of strength, flavor, and hoppiness. American brown ales tend to be more bitter than their English counterparts and fall somewhere between English porters and English brown ales on the flavor spectrum. American browns tend to be very food-friendly and can be paired with a wide variety of cuisine.

Color: These are aptly named: most brown ales are either light, dark, or medium brown, with possible reddish undertones.

Flavor: Due to their darker color, roasted malt flavors are stronger in brown ales. Some have deep, almost stout-like chocolate and coffee flavors, and most are decidedly low in fruity notes.

Alcohol content: Between 4 and 8 percent

Bitterness: Between 25 and 45 IBU, on average

Glass: Nonic pint or shaker pint

Examples: Brooklyn Brown Ale, Brooklyn Brewery; Hazelnut Brown Nectar, Rogue Ales; Moose Drool Brown Ale, Big Sky Brewing

American Black Ale

Also called black IPA or Cascadian dark ale, beers in this style have a distinctive mix of caramelly, roasted malt flavor and fruity, citrusy hops. The hops make these beers, with each variety imparting unique floral and/or herbal notes to the end brew; like barleywines, black ales are not for the weak of palate.

Color: Black ales can be anywhere from a deep, dark brown to almost completely black. Fewer styles are darker than these beers.

Flavor: These beers are aggressive in both hoppy bitterness and roasted malt flavors, which is characteristic to the style; if you're opting for a black ale, you're not looking for a mild brew.

Alcohol content: Between 5 and 10 percent

Bitterness: Between 50 and 70 IBU, on average

Glass: Snifter or tulip

Examples: Dark Penance, Founders Brewing Company; Iniquity (Imperial Black Ale), Southern Tier Brewing Company; NightTime, Lagunitas Brewing Company

American Pale Ale

One of the American craft-beer movement's flagship styles, the American pale ale (APA)—like most American styles of beer—is a variant of a European (in this case, British) original. Commonly brewed using Cascade hops, APAs tend to have more of a balance between their hop and malt flavors, unlike India pale ales (IPAs), which are assertively hoppier, although some breweries blur the line. If you're looking for a balanced, classic brew, an American pale ale may be right up your alley.

Color: APAs are a pale golden color.

Flavor: More balanced than IPAs, these beers can be mild to moderately fruity and are usually decently hoppy and bitter, especially if brewed with Cascade hops. They also tend to have clean, uncomplicated flavors.

Alcohol content: Anywhere between 4 and 7 percent

Bitterness: Between 30 and 50 IBU, on average

Glass: Shaker pint or tulip

Examples: Doggie Style Classic Pale Ale, 3 Floyds Brewing Company; Headwaters Pale Ale, Victory Brewing Company; Sierra Nevada Pale Ale, Sierra Nevada Brewing Company

American Wheat

An American take on the German hefeweizen, these beers are brewed with different yeasts to avoid the banana and clove flavors usually present in German wheat beers. Like most American riffs on other styles, these wheat beers tend to be hoppier than their European counterparts. Most are also unfiltered, so they pour cloudy from the bottle.

Color: The color can range from pale straw to light amber.

Flavor: Ideal for the summer, these beers can range in hop flavor considerably but tend not to be very bitter. Their considerable percentage of wheat malts lends them light and fruity flavors.

Alcohol content: Anywhere between 3.5 and 7 percent

Bitterness: Between 10 and 35 IBU, on average

Glass: Shaker pint or weizen

Examples: 312 Urban Wheat, Goose Island Brewing Company; A Little Sumpin' Sumpin' Ale, Lagunitas Brewing Company; Samuel Adams Coastal Wheat, Boston Beer Company

Blonde Ale

Blonde ales are eminently approachable. The style is another sort of catchall, but its main defining feature is its lack of dominating malt and hop characteristics. Also known as golden ales, these beers are well-balanced and can be brewed with honey, fruits, and spices for added individuality. Their colors tend to be very similar to those of American pale ales but without the considerable hoppiness of those brews.

Color: Blonde ales typically range from pale straw to light gold.

Flavor: It's tough to detail a specific flavor common to blonde ales, but most are not overly hoppy and almost lager-like. They are light-bodied and simple, although the additions of fruits and spices can add to their complexity.

Alcohol content: Between 4 and 7 percent

Bitterness: Between 15 and 25 IBU, on average

Glass: Shaker pint or tulip

Examples: Aud Blonde, Russian River Brewing Company; Big Wave Golden Ale, Kona Brewing Company; Bombshell Blonde, Southern Star Brewing Company

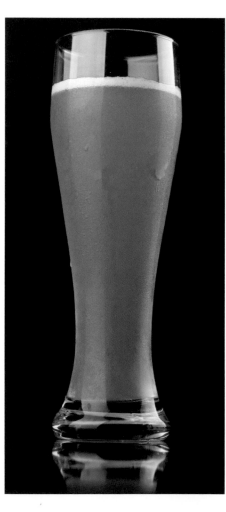

Hefeweizen

With *weizen* meaning "wheat" and the prefix *hefe-* meaning "with yeast" in German, the hefeweizen's name quickly becomes clear: this style of beer is German in origin, brewed with a majority of malted wheat, and served unfiltered, meaning that a hefeweizen looks cloudy in your glass because of the presence of yeast. American wheat beers are riffs on hefeweizens, but these beers get their distinctive flavors—banana and clove, mainly, although some beer aficionados have mentioned bubblegum and spice flavors, too—from the strains of yeast used to brew them. Darker German wheat-based beers with additional malt flavors are known as *dunkelweizens*, and filtered hefeweizens are called *kristalweizens*.

Color: The high wheat content imparts a color that ranges from pale straw to amber.

Flavor: Hefeweizens are very low in hop flavors and aromas as well as bitterness. Additionally, the style tends to have long-lasting rings of foam that remain at the top of the glass.

Alcohol content: Between 4 and 6 percent

Bitterness: 10 and 15 IBU, on average

Glass: Weizen

Examples: Ebel's Weiss, Two Brothers Brewing Company; In-Heat Wheat, Flying Dog Brewery; Live Oak Hefeweizen, Live Oak Brewing Company

India Pale Ale

The American pale ale may be one of the American craft-beer movement's flagship styles, but the style that has truly thrived in the last several decades is the American India pale ale, or IPA. In fact, CraftBeer.com notes that American IPAs have been the most-entered style at the Great American Beer festival for more than a decade and that it is also the top-selling craft beer style at supermarkets and liquor stores across the country. Spun off from English IPAs, American IPAs are all about those hops—no playing. Most IPAs will hit you in the nose and tongue with floral, piney, citrusy hop aroma and flavor and the bitterness to match. They're definitely an acquired taste, but most aficionados say that once you go for the hops, you never look back.

> **Color:** Similar in color to American pale ales, IPAs range from pale gold to medium amber.
>
> **Flavor:** IPAs are all about the hops, with citrus and floral notes up front and piney and herbal endnotes.
>
> **Alcohol content:** Anywhere between 5.5 and 7.5 percent
>
> **Bitterness:** Between 50 and 70 IBU, on average
>
> **Glass:** Shaker pint or tulip
>
> **Examples:** Deviant Dale's IPA, Oskar Blues Grill and Brew; Founders All Day IPA, Founders Brewing Company; Two Hearted Ale, Bell's Brewery, Inc.

Irish Red Ale

Similar to American red and amber ales, Irish red ales are basically medium across the board—not that there's anything wrong with that. They're medium-colored and medium-bodied and tend to have a medium hoppiness. Their defining characteristic is a toasted malty sweetness, and—surprise, surprise—it's a medium level of sweetness that's balanced by a dry, hoppy finish. If you're looking for a beer to offer you the middle of the road of the craft-beer movement, an Irish red won't lead you astray.

> **Color:** True to their name, Irish reds are light to dark red.
>
> **Flavor:** This style is known for its prevailing sweetness with notes of caramel and toffee and hoppy endnotes.
>
> **Alcohol content:** Between 4 and 6 percent
>
> **Bitterness:** Between 20 and 28 IBU, on average
>
> **Glass:** Nonic pint or shaker pint
>
> **Examples:** Great Lakes Conway's Irish Ale, Great Lakes Brewing Company; Lucky S.O.B., Flying Dog Brewery; O'Hara's Irish Red, Carlow Brewing Company

Porter

One of the darker styles of beer, porter has its roots in eighteenth-century England, where the dark and well-hopped brews were popular with London's transportation workers. In fact, the style name is said to have come from those porters themselves. Today, these robust beers are commonly flavored with coffee and chocolate to accentuate their roasted malt character, and the style also lends itself well to bourbon-barrel aging.

Color: Porters range from dark brown to black; they are usually, but not always, slightly lighter in color than stouts.

Flavor: This style brings a strong roasted malt flavor, though not as strong as that of stouts.

Alcohol content: Between 5 and 7.5 percent

Bitterness: Between 25 and 40 IBU, on average

Glass: Nonic pint or shaker pint

Examples: Alaskan Smoked Porter, Alaskan Brewing Company; Evil Twin Lil' B, Evil Twin Brewing Company; Great Lakes Edmund Fitzgerald Porter, Great Lakes Brewing Company

Saison

The saison style originated in Belgium and shares similar characteristics with many other famous styles from that country: lightish in flavor, golden in color, and with yeasty notes giving the beer a slightly cloudy bottle appearance (saisons are commonly unfiltered). Saisons are also called farmhouse ales in the United States, and they're commonly brewed in the winter but intended for drinking in the summer. Most are significantly fruity and complex although they're not necessarily hopped heavily. Many are also brewed with specific herbs and spices that give them a distinctive character.

Color: Saisons range from pale to deep gold.

Flavor: This style features a lot of spicy, fruity notes with minimal sweetness and moderate bitterness.

Alcohol content: Between 5 and 8 percent

Bitterness: Between 20 and 40 IBU, on average

Glass: Tulip

Examples: Hennepin, Brewery Ommegang; Rabbid Rabbit, 3 Floyds Brewing Company; Sofie, Goose Island Beer Company

Scotch Ale

Unsurprisingly, given their name, Scotch ales originate from Scotland, and they are one of the major Scottish styles in America today. Also sometimes referred to as "wee heavy," Scotch ales are most known for their heavy maltiness, which results in a full-bodied and complex beer with a variety of sweet flavor notes—think caramel and roasted malt. To achieve this caramelly malt flavor, beers in this style are commonly boiled for longer than most to slightly caramelize the wort. Some versions also incorporate a smoky flavor.

Color: Scotch ales range from reddish-brown to deep brown.

Flavor: Predominantly malty, this style offers considerable sweetness and minimal hoppiness.

Alcohol content: Between 6 and 10 percent

Bitterness: Between 25 and 35 IBU, on average

Glass: Thistle

Examples: Jinx, Magic Hat Brewing Company; Old Chub, Oskar Blues Grill and Brew; Wee Heavy-er Scotch Style Ale, French Broad Brewing Company

Stout

This dark, rich brew started as an offshoot of its closest style kin, the porter: the strongest porters that a brewery would offer became known as "stout porters," which was eventually shortened to just "stout." America, England, and Ireland all have variants on this style: American stouts are bold and bitter, especially in their finishes, and hoppier than their counterparts; English stouts are defined mainly by their extreme use of roasted barley in the grain bill, and it's usually roasted to the point of charring; and Irish stouts are a lower-carbonation creation, with hop levels that average in between American and English varieties. Think of stouts as porters with the dial turned up to 9 or 10.

Color: Beers don't get darker than stouts, which range from deep brown to pitch black.

Flavor: Deep, rich, and strong with abounding coffee and chocolate notes, most stouts have an unmistakable roasted character.

Alcohol content: Between 4 and 8 percent

Bitterness: Between 35 and 60 IBU, on average

Glass: Shaker pint or tulip

Examples: Obsidian Stout, Deschutes Brewery; Out of Bounds Stout, Avery Brewing Company; Steelhead Extra Stout, Mad River Brewing Company

Winter Warmer

There's arguably no better beer to drink during the winter holidays than a winter warmer. These malt-forward beers are commonly flavored with warming spices, such as cinnamon, nutmeg, and ginger, and are usually hop-light in both flavor and perceived bitterness. English versions of this style are commonly brewed without added spices, instead opting for a beer that lands between a brown ale and a porter. Both the spiced and unspiced versions will keep you warm on those cold winter nights—this style tends to lean higher on the ABV spectrum.

Color: Winter warmers are seen in colors that range from dark amber to dark brown.

Flavor: The flavors vary considerably, depending on the spices used, but the style is usually malty and sweet with little to no bitterness.

Alcohol content: Between 5.5 and 8 percent

Bitterness: Between 5 and 40 IBU, on average

Glass: Shaker pint

Examples: Great Lakes Christmas Ale, Great Lakes Brewing Company; Mogul Madness Ale, Rogue Ales; Redhook Winterhook, Redhook Ale Brewery

Witbier

Translating to "white beer," the witbier style gets its name from its pale color, which it owes to the high level of wheat (and occasionally oats) in the grain bill. These Belgian-style beers are frequently spiced with coriander and orange peel, and most breweries try to set their creations apart from the crowd with additional seasonings. These beers, like their hefeweizen kin, are unfiltered, and their yeast remains suspended in the end product.

Color: Witbiers are incredibly pale and cloudy.

Flavor: This style is known for an exceptionally low hop flavoring and bitterness, having a crisp, citrusy, and spicy tang.

Alcohol content: Between 4 and 6 percent

Bitterness: Between 10 and 17 IBU, on average

Glass: Pilsner or shaker pint

Examples: Namaste, Dogfish Head Brewery; Whirlwind Witbier, Victory Brewing Company; White Rascal, Avery Brewing Company

Lagers

More specialized than ales, lagers are the backbone of American beer. Don't be swayed by your past experiences with the mass offerings from the macrobreweries—lagers more than hold their own against their ale cousins.

American Amber Lager

Like its sister category, the American amber ale, this is a catchall category for all of the American-style lagers that have additional character and body than their pale American lager cousins. Widely available and incredibly popular, larger breweries tend to produce this style more than the smaller craft breweries.

Color: This style ranges in color from pale to dark amber.

Flavor: Hoppiness is typically nonexistent to moderate, and the style features a lager-esque crispness with a malty backbone.

Alcohol content: Between 4 and 6 percent

Bitterness: Between 18 and 30 IBU, on average

Glass: Shaker pint or pilsner

Examples: Leinenkugel's Classic Amber, Jacob Leinenkugel Brewing Company; Samuel Adams Boston Lager, Boston Beer Company; Yuengling Traditional Lager, Yuengling Brewery

American Pale Lager

The most popular style of beer in America (and the world), American pale lagers make up the majority of offerings from the macrobreweries. Low in malts, they typically use considerable cereal adjuncts, such as rice and corn, in their grain bills. A subset of this style is known as light lager, which is where you'll find Bud Light, Miller Lite, and Coors Light. Some craft breweries do riff on these crisp, light, and refreshing beers, but most leave the pale lagers to the big boys.

Color: Pale lagers are—you guessed it—pale in color.

Flavor: Pale lagers are very low in malt flavor and have a crisp, dry, and light body.

Alcohol content: Between 3 and 5 percent

Bitterness: Between 8 and 20 IBU, on average

Glass: Pilsner

Examples: Light, Abita Brewing Company; Longboard Island Lager, Kona Brewing Company; Totally Naked, New Glarus Brewing Company

Bock

The origin of these German all-malt brews is a little fuzzy, but *bock* directly translates to "goat," so those ornery farm animals were likely involved somewhere in the naming process. Thankfully, these sweet beers don't taste goaty at all; rather, they're decidedly nut-like in their malty flavors, and the caramel notes common to other malt-forward beers are absent here. These lagers tend to be stronger than their other lager relatives and are only lightly hopped, mainly to balance the sweetness of the malts. There are several substyles: *eisbock*, a high-alcohol variety that achieves its signature strength by freezing the brew after fermentation and removing some of the water content; *dopplebock*, meaning "double bock," a variety with even more malt flavor that is reminiscent of toasted bread; *maibock*, a lighter, more heavily hopped variety typically served in the spring; and *weizenbock*, a bock made with wheat that winds up tasting like a lager version of a dunkelweizen.

Color: Bocks range in color from dark amber to dark brown.

Flavor: Malt-forward with a heavy but balanced sweetness; typically, a hop flavor is almost unnoticeable, unless you're drinking a maibock.

Alcohol content: Anywhere between 5.5 and 7.5 percent

Bitterness: Between 20 and 30 IBU, on average

Glass: Stange or pilsner

Examples: Anchor Bock Beer, Anchor Brewing Company; Bock Beer, Rivertown Brewing Company; Uff-da, New Glarus Brewing Company

Dunkel

Sometimes called a Munich dunkel or Münchner dunkel, this is a German lager that uses specific Munich dark malt to give it a characteristic bready, biscuity flavor and a dark, reddish color—*dunkel* translates to "dark." The style is not often very sweet; it's hopped moderately, and the resulting impression is a well-balanced, complex beer with a rich, full body. Brewers achieve the characteristic flavor through the use of the aforementioned Munich dark malts as well as through a technique called *decoction mashing*, which is uncommon to almost all other styles of beer. In decoction mashing, some of the grains are boiled and then returned to the wort, raising the temperature and causing more starch to be extracted from the grain, leading to those characteristic dunkel flavor notes.

Color: The color varies from light to dark brown, often with considerable red.

Flavor: The malty but balanced flavor features strong notes of chocolate, bread, and biscuits.

Alcohol content: Between 4 and 5.5 percent; it rarely goes above 5.5 percent

Bitterness: Between 16 and 25 IBU, on average

Glass: Pilsner

Examples: Capital Dark, Capital Brewery; Harpoon Dark, Harpoon Brewery & Beer Hall; Victory Dark Lager, Victory Brewing Company

Helles

The dunkel's light-colored sibling in name, *helles* translates to "pale," and the style was thusly named to distinguish it from the darker-hued dunkel. Similar in flavor to a pilsner, helles are usually a little bit sweeter and drier in finish, as well as slightly maltier. They are not heavily hopped, instead focusing on barley flavors and mild, bready notes. CraftBeer.com calls the helles a "refreshing beer with substance."

> **Color:** As the style's name suggests, helles ranges from pale to medium gold.
>
> **Flavor:** The brew is light on hoppy bitterness and flavor, with a crisp, clean finish and a slightly sweet, bready body.
>
> **Alcohol content:** Between 4 and 5.5 percent
>
> **Bitterness:** Between 18 and 25 IBU, on average
>
> **Glass:** Pilsner
>
> **Examples:** Bikini Blonde Lager, Maui Brewing Company; Gorch Fock, 3 Floyds Brewing Company; Penn Gold, Pennsylvania Brewing Company

Märzen/Oktoberfest

Before refrigeration, beer brewing in the summer was almost impossible. The warm temperatures would just wreak havoc on the brews, and bacteria would run rampant. As such, the brewing season would typically take a hiatus during hotter weather, so the final beers brewed in the spring were kept in cold storage and cracked open for the Oktoberfest celebrations in the fall. Those beers take their two names from the month of the year in which they're brewed (*Märzen* is German for "March") and the festival (Oktoberfest) at which they're enjoyed in the fall. These beers are full-bodied and rich, with malty notes, considerable hop aroma and flavor, and a medium to high alcohol content.

> **Color:** Oktoberfest beers range from light brown to deep, reddish brown.
>
> **Flavor:** The toasted malt flavor has balanced bitterness and a clean, dry finish.
>
> **Alcohol content:** Between 5 and 7 percent
>
> **Bitterness:** Between 18 and 25 IBU, on average
>
> **Glass:** Shaker pint or mug
>
> **Examples:** Great Lakes Oktoberfest, Great Lakes Brewing Company; Left Hand Oktoberfest, Left Hand Brewing Company; SurlyFest, Surly Brewing Company

Pilsner

Another of the world's most common beer styles, the pilsner—sometimes spelled pilsener—is light and crisp with a residual malt sweetness. Some pilsners are citrusy and floral, while some are spicy and grassy, but all of them are moderately to heavily hopped. Originating in the Czech Republic, the Czech version of the style is a bit more aggressive than the German varieties, with occasional yeast flavors that come through.

Color: Pilsners range in color from pale straw to pale gold.

Flavor: Moderately hoppy flavors feature spicy and floral notes and a dense, rich head.

Alcohol content: Between 4 and 5.5 percent

Bitterness: Between 25 and 40 IBU, on average

Glass: Pilsner

Examples: Nooner Pilsner, Sierra Nevada Brewing Company; SOS (Save Our Shore), Abita Brewing Company; Tröegs Sunshine Pilsner, Tröegs Brewing Company

Schwarzbier

Similar to the dunkel, the *schwarzbier*—German for "black beer"—style is a dark, almost black, lager with strong chocolate and coffee flavors. (Dunkels tend to be more roast-flavored than schwarzbiers, which is the main differences between the styles.) Still decidedly light beers, these make excellent choices if you're looking for summer brews that are a little more substantial and full-bodied than other lagers.

Color: True to its name, the schwarzbier style ranges from deep brown to black.

Flavor: The strong coffee and chocolate flavors are accompanied by a mild malt sweetness.

Alcohol content: Between 4 and 5.5 percent

Bitterness: Between 22 and 30 IBU, on average

Glass: Pilsner

Examples: Black Thunder, Austin Beerworks; Howl, Magic Hat Brewing Company; Rail Dog Smoked Black Lager, Thirsty Dog Brewing Company

Hybrid Beers

Not quite lagers and not quite ales, these hybrid beers fall somewhere in between. Whether they're brewed with a mix of yeast styles or at unusual temperatures, these combo beers straddle the line betwcen lagers and ales with delicious results.

California Common

A uniquely American style, California common beers (or steam beers as they were originally known), fall somewhere between ales and lagers: they're brewed with lager yeasts but fermented at warmer temperatures, resulting in a beer with malty notes and a mild fruitiness. They're almost exclusively hopped with a strain called Northern Brewer, which lends the final product a woodsy, almost piney flavor—some fans can also detect notes of mint. Common in the 1800s before refrigeration was widespread, San Francisco's Anchor Brewing Company rescued the style from obscurity and has trademarked the term "steam beer" today.

Color: California commons run from light to medium amber.

Flavor: This is an assertively hoppy style with piney notes but also a balancing malty flavor.

Alcohol content: Between 4 and 6 percent

Bitterness: Between 35 and 45 IBU, on average

Glass: Nonic pint or pilsner

Examples: Anchor Steam, Anchor Brewing Company; Fullsteam, Fullsteam Brewery; Schlafly Pi Common, The Schlafly Tap Room

Imperials

Check out the beer offerings at your local liquor store or beer distributor, and you're bound to see some of the beer styles listed in this chapter with the word "imperial" in front of their names: imperial stouts, imperial IPAs, imperial pilsners...the list goes on. The "imperial" designation isn't just to make the name sound fancier; it actually signifies that the beer is stronger and more intense than its counterparts.

Stemming from the nineteenth century, the term "imperial" came about to describe English beers–typically stouts–that were exported to Russia's imperial court. These beers were the cream of the crop, stronger than most other brews, with additional flavor and complexity. Over the years, and especially in today's American craft-beer scene, the term has come to mean a bold, intense take on a beer style, usually with considerably more hops and malts and a much higher ABV. It's not unheard of for imperial stouts to clock in at 15 percent ABV!

If you like the standard take on a style, give an imperial version a try when you're feeling adventurous. They're definitely amped up, and you'll likely pay more for less beer, but they're almost always worth the price. Just don't be surprised if the beers bite back!

Cream Ale

No, these beers aren't actually brewed with any dairy products; rather, these classic American beers are a spinoff of American lagers. They're usually light and refreshing, and they tend to combine characteristics from both the lager and ale families of beer—they're brewed as ales but can be finished as lagers. (Some people even consider cream ales to be ale/lager hybrids.) Most cream ales also use adjuncts such as rice or corn in the brewing process to further lighten the body, but some commercial breweries also produce all-malt versions.

Color: Cream ales can range from pale straw to pale gold.

Flavor: Cream ales, like American lagers, are clean, crisp, and very easy to drink. Hop and malt flavors are muted, and the style tends to be well carbonated.

Alcohol content: Anywhere between 4 and 7 percent

Bitterness: Between 10 and 22 IBU, on average

Glass: Shaker pint or flute

Examples: Spotted Cow, New Glarus Brewing Company; Summer Solstice, Anderson Valley Brewing Company; Sunlight Cream Ale, Sun King Brewing Company

Kölsch

Originally brewed only in Köln, Germany, the kölsch is brewed with top-fermenting ale yeasts and then conditioned at lager temperatures, resulting in a very light-colored beer with a dry, crisp finish. Although relatively obscure a few decades ago, the American craft-beer movement took heavily to kölsch-style beers, and a larger number of breweries currently offer brews based on this German traditional style.

Color: Kölsch brews range from pale straw to pale gold.

Flavor: Light in malt flavor and usually medium-bodied, these beers have a medium level of hoppiness with a dry, almost wine-like finish.

Alcohol content: Between 4.5 and 6 percent

Bitterness: Between 18 and 28 IBU, on average

Glass: Stange

Examples: Kmita Kölsch, Dark Horse Brewing Company; Kölsch, Bluegrass Brewing Company; New Holland Full Circle, New Holland Brewing Company

Beer Glasses

To best experience these beer styles, drink them in glasses that best accentuate their flavors, aromas, and nuances. It may seem as if a glass is a glass is a glass, but taste a German lager out of a regular pint glass and then out of a pilsner glass--as it's intended to be consumed--and you'll be surprised how much more the beer comes alive in a pilsner. If you've taken the time to brew your own beer, don't do yourself the disservice of serving it in the wrong glass.

A good portion of the taste and aroma differences between serving vessels comes from the presence (or lack thereof) of volatile organic compounds (or just "volatiles" or VOCs, for short). These compounds are the molecules that evaporate from beer to give each brew its signature aroma, and they include hop oils; flavoring agents like herbs, fruits, and spices; and fermentation by-products like esters and fusels.

It may seem counterintuitive, but the head that forms when you pour your beer can actually help you discern the brew's true flavor and aroma--that head helps trap some of the volatiles as they escape from your glass, concentrating the beer's aroma for your first several sips. *Beer Advocate* magazine recommends a head of 1-1.5 inches for most beers to best facilitate the proper taste experience.

Some glasses are also designed to showcase a beer's color or carbonation level. Others are designed to incorporate the warmth of your hand as you drink, while still others have been engineered to stay cool or hold less beer--both of these styles are intended to keep the beer at the optimum serving temperature for as long as possible.

This guide gives you more information on the various styles of beer glasses and how they enhance or accentuate beers consumed from them. (Note: This is merely a guide to the major glass types. Many breweries in Europe take beer glasses so seriously that they will engineer a specific glass for each brand of beer that they serve. If that isn't enough evidence to prove to you that glasses are important, I don't know what is!)

Beer Glasses

Flute: These long and slender stemmed glasses—very similar, if not identical to, champagne flutes—allow the beers they hold to maintain their carbonation longer while also showcasing a beer's color and lacing (the leftover foam on the side of the glass after you take a drink). Flutes are best for Belgian-style beers that have complex, heady aromas because they help concentrate volatiles at the narrow top of the glass. Try German and Belgian lagers, as well as lambics, in flutes.

Mug: Mugs are arguably one of the most iconic serving vessels for beer, and they're certainly the best for toasting—their thick walls make them very difficult to break. Those same thick walls also keep beer cold longer, as does the handle, which keeps the drinker's warm hand away from the cold glass body. They come in a wide variety of sizes and shapes, and because they have such a large holding capacity, mugs lend themselves well to lower ABV beers. You can drink most any style of beer out of a mug, but German, American, and English ales may taste the best.

Nonic Pint: A variant on the more common shaker pint, the nonic pint is slightly larger, usually able to hold 20 ounces of beer, and is designed to be easier to stack and grip. This glass is ideal for beers with considerable heads, as the increased size allows the head to fully develop, while the shaker pint can restrict the heads on some beers. Ales of all types, stouts, and porters—especially English styles because that's where the glass originated—are excellent out of a nonic pint. Tulip pints are similar in size and shape to the nonic pint, and can be used for similar beers.

Pilsner: Ideal for pale lagers and (not surprisingly) pilsners, these tall, tapered glasses promote head retention and show off the sparkling colors and carbonation of the beers inside them. A true pilsner glass has no amount of curvature to it at all and is usually smaller than a regular pint glass because pale lagers are meant to be consumed at cooler temperatures. A pokal is a pilsner glass with a slight stem at the bottom.

Shaker Pint: When in doubt, choose the shaker pint. This smooth, slightly tapered, conical glass style is simple, unfettered, and easily stackable, grippable, and washable. It doesn't really do anything special in terms of highlighting volatiles or promoting head retention, but its wide mouth allows for deep sips, and no beer is going to taste bad coming out of it. As with nonic pints, ales are best suited for shaker pints; on the whole, lagers benefit from specialized glassware.

Snifter: Snifters are designed for beers that have complex flavors and contain significant amounts of volatiles, such as barleywines, imperial stouts, IPAs, and bocks. Their size varies, but they're designed to allow drinkers to swirl and agitate the beer inside, promoting the release of these flavor and aroma compounds that are then funneled to the glass's narrow head. The bowl of the glass is meant to fit snugly in the drinker's hand, allowing it to warm up the beer slightly, further promoting the release of the valuable volatiles. These glasses are also used for brandy and cognac, which should be enjoyed in a similar way.

Stange: Designed specifically for the German kölsch and altbier, these straight-sided cylinders are smaller than traditional pint glasses, intending to encourage drinkers to drink quickly, as these beers are best consumed cold. The tight shape keeps volatiles concentrated, and if you're unable to get your hands on one, a Tom Collins glass will work in a pinch.

Stein: Steins are very similar to mugs, with one major difference: they have a hinged lid that is opened with a thumb lever. It's suggested that these lids came about during the Black Plague, when beer drinkers wanted a way to keep flies out of their brews. Where a mug will work, so will a stein, although German beers are probably best suited to steins as a tip of the hat to the glass's country of origin.

Thistle: Thistle glasses are really used only for Scotch ales and occasionally barleywines, and the style takes its name from its resemblance to the thistle blossom. The bulb at the bottom is ideal for allowing the drinker's hand to gently warm the beer, while the tapered and flared top half concentrates and then releases the beer's aroma. This style is similar in appearance to the tulip glass.

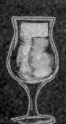

Tulip: Not to be confused with tulip pint glasses, tulip glasses look like less-exaggerated thistle glasses, and they accomplish similar goals: the bulbous body allows the beer to warm from contact with hands while the flared top concentrates and then releases volatiles. Unlike thistle glasses, however, tulips are great for serving almost any aromatic beers. Most Belgian styles, IPAs, pale ales, and even Scotch ales and barleywines are enhanced by this attractive glassware.

Weizen: German for "wheat," curvy weizen glasses are ideal for wheat beers: they promote head retention with their tapered bottoms and wide-mouthed tops, their height allows the head to flourish, and the tapered bottom also helps trap yeast sediment, keeping it from deflating the beer's head but still allowing those trademark flavors to come through. Try a weizen glass for your hefeweizens and their variants, along with any other wheat beers, regardless of country of origin.

8

Batch Diary

I don't know about you, but I learn best by example. When I brewed my first batch of beer, I had already attended an introductory class at my local home-brew supply store, and I had done some very basic research, so I had an idea what I was getting myself into. However, I knew that I wasn't truly going to get a handle on home brewing until I got my hands dirty, so to speak—and get my hands dirty, I did.

After that first batch, I knew what to be prepared for (and just exactly how long it was going to take that bubbling pot of wort to cool without a wort chiller), and I was much better equipped to handle subsequent batches. The specifics no longer seemed so vague and confusing, and I had concrete ideas of what to expect from all aspects of the process.

So here's the next best thing: a step-by-step, day-by-day diary of The Little Jerry pale ale that I brewed while writing this book. You'll get the good, the bad, and the ugly of the home-brew process firsthand, from deciding on which style to brew to detailed accounts of the brewing and bottling processes, complete with the reasoning behind every decision (including an explanation of what the heck that name means!). My hopes are that you'll be able to read this chapter and come out significantly more prepared for the nervous excitement that accompanies your first home-brewed batch of beer, whatever it may be.

Amber bottles best protect your brew from degradation.

Saturday, March 7

We began preliminary discussions on this batch today. When I home brew, I always do so with my best friend and roommate, Dustin. We call our little operation Mother Hen Brewing, after a long and storied history of chicken jokes, songs, and idiocies from our youth (all of which still occur now—who am I kidding?). We knew that this batch would be spotlighted in this book, so we wanted to put a little more thought into deciding on style than we have in the past; usually, we just base our batches on what time of year we're brewing and what would be most seasonally appropriate.

Our beer tastes definitely come into play as well. My favorite beers are dark, malty, roasty porters and stouts, while Dustin—"Dut" for short—usually opts for citrusy, aggressively hoppy IPAs. That's not to say that our tastes don't overlap at all; rather, if we're going to spend the time and money on a batch, we just want it to be a style that we both happily agree on. Because of this, our very first batch was an Oktoberfest, and we've also done an IPA and a porter.

Because the American pale ale not only is one of the flagship beers of the American craft-beer movement but also is quite easy to brew, this style became an early frontrunner in our discussion. We also tossed around the idea of an oatmeal stout, but because this style requires extra steps that are a little beyond the skill level of beginner home brewers—and ones that we've never tried at all—we decided to keep that one on the back burner. We also liked the idea of tipping the hat to our adopted state of Kentucky and our mutual love of bourbon by brewing something that used bourbon-barrel pieces, but that one also moved quickly to the on-deck circle.

After continued deliberation and a frank discussion about our existing equipment, we decided to plunge ahead with the pale ale. It just seemed to be the best option, given the stipulations that we were dealing with. The style's middle-of-the-road flavors and easy drinkability meant that most of our friends would happily accept a gift of several bottles whenever we stopped by their houses. Sure, home brewing is intended to be cost-effective, but when you give away half of a batch like we tend to, those ingredient costs don't usually even out. Granted, the list of people who want to try our batches of beer keeps growing, so we're clearly doing something right.

We've always fermented in a carboy before, but it can be a bit ungainly to clean and move around, especially when it's full of fermenting wort. This time, we decided to brew

With tastes on opposite ends of the spectrum, we first had to agree on what style to brew.

in a fermenting bucket. Portability was definitely a factor in the decision, as was the simple desire for a change. One of the major downsides to brewing in a bucket over a glass carboy is the lack of visibility—with a carboy, you get a front-row seat to all of the bubbling action while the beer ferments, while the opaque bucket allows you to see only the bubbles escaping the airlock, leaving you in a bit more suspense. Nonetheless, we decided to forge ahead with the bucket.

Our First Batch

Allow me to clarify slightly: our first batch was intended to be an Oktoberfest, but because we didn't have temperature-control abilities in our tiny apartment at the time, it technically turned out to be an amber ale. We tried to keep frozen bottles of water on the fermenting vessel to lower the temperature as much as we could, but we never got it below 60 degrees Fahrenheit. The beer was eminently drinkable, though, so you didn't hear either of us complaining.

Bourbon-Barrel Ale

If you're not familiar with the bourbon-distilling process, the spirit is aged in a charred white-oak barrel and pulls its amber color and some of its flavor from the barrel itself. Distilleries sell these barrels—and, more affordable and practical for us, pieces of charred barrels—to the public for further use. Adding these pieces of used barrel imparts smooth notes of toffee and vanilla, as well as a slight bourbon flavor, to a beer. We're still coming for you, bourbon-barrel ale. Don't you worry.

Monday, March 16

We decided to purchase a wort chiller with this batch. It's an optional piece of equipment, but we thought that cooling the wort in our kitchen sink was just taking too much time. Brew day requires only a few hours of time, but if we could cut out half an hour for just a small investment, we thought that it would be worth it. Our brewing supplies are pretty basic as they stand, so we decided that a wort chiller would be a smart addition.

We opted for an immersion model that connects to the kitchen sink. You place the brew pot in the sink after the boil is finished, connect the wort chiller to the faucet, submerge the (sanitized) metal tubing into the hot wort, and turn on the faucet. The cold water that flows through the tubing cools the wort to room temperature significantly faster than the ice bath we'd used for previous batches.

We decided to go the immersion route because it was the most cost-effective (despite being the least water-efficient) wort chiller variety. The water waste during the 5 minutes of wort chilling is excessive at best, since you're just basically running the faucet for an extended period of time; that said, immersion chillers are one of the most efficient ways to quickly cool a batch of just-boiled wort.

There are some concerns with immersion wort chillers giving the beer a metallic taste in the end, but we decided to take that risk. As far as metal choices go, stainless steel is a little more expensive on average and is definitely easier to clean, but we opted for copper and its speedier cooling. Our major concern was the potential for oxides to form on the coils after use, which could alter the flavor of the beer in a negative way, but the cheaper price and the faster cool time swayed us in the end. We figured that we'd just make sure to clean the coils thoroughly after use.

Pale ale appeals to a wide range of beer drinkers.

Wednesday, March 25

The wort chiller arrived today. Dut volunteered to hook the chiller up and test for leaks, which was fine by me—I must admit that plumbing and waterline issues are not among my strong suits. Our model came with a faucet adapter, which was another reason we chose it over some of the others—not having to involve a separate room of the apartment (i.e., the bathroom) seemed like a wise idea. The connections between the plastic tubing that attached to the copper coils did prove to have very slight leaks– just a drip every several seconds or so—but otherwise, it seemed to be working admirably. We elected to just hold a

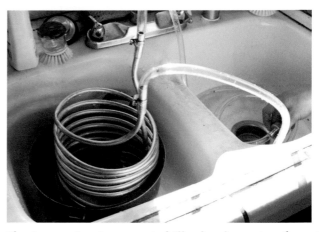

The immersion-type wort chiller hooks up to a faucet.

towel by those loose connections while the faucet was running to keep the occasional drips from falling into the wort. We could have probably jury-rigged a fix of some kind, but it didn't seem worth the effort, especially when the easier fix was just keeping the drips from hitting the wort.

Wednesday, April 1: Shopping Day

We went shopping for ingredients at our local liquor store/home-brew supply store tonight. The store is called Liquor Barn, and despite having lived in Kentucky for nearly five years and frequenting this store since my first week as a Kentucky resident, I can't help but smile when I think about the name. Liquor Warehouse would be a more appropriate name, honestly. The store is enormous, carrying thousands of beer, wine, and liquor varieties in addition to a full range of home-brewing and wine-making supplies, not to mention the deli and the multiple taps where you can get an exceedingly affordable growler fill.

Anyway, I digress. To Liquor Barn we went, looking to purchase all of the ingredients we'd need for The Little Jerry pale ale. We were also buying a few additional pieces of equipment: a brew bucket without a spigot at the bottom, a sturdier spoon (preferably metal), and a stick-on thermometer for the brew bucket. The latter was slightly unnecessary,

Shopping List

I realize that a list of purchased ingredients and equipment is a little boring, but it's pretty indicative of what you're in for if you choose to brew a batch of beer without using a starter kit. You have to be meticulous in your shopping to avoid finding yourself halfway through a boil only to discover that you're an ounce of hops short or that you've forgotten an important piece of equipment.

but we wanted one just in case we decided to brew any lagers in the future. We figured it would be a good investment; plus, it's never a bad idea to keep an eye on the temperature of your fermenting beer.

Thankfully, we had no issues finding what we needed at Liquor Barn. We picked up 6 pounds of dry light malt extract, a pound of Crystal 20L malt grains, a pound of American 6-row malt grains, 2

Cascade hops were among the ingredients for our pale ale.

ounces of Centennial hops, 2 ounces of Cascade hops, and a package of Safale US-05 yeast. In addition, we grabbed a bottle of Iodophor (our supply was running low) and a steeping bag for the grains. Equipment-wise, we snagged the aforementioned spigotless brewing bucket with a grommeted lid, a sturdy metal spoon, and a thermometer sticker as well as a measurement tube for our hydrometer, which we've never properly used, despite our best efforts. (Spoiler alert: we weren't using enough of the wort and fermented beer to take our original and final gravity readings.)

Of course, what visit to the brewing-supply store would be complete without picking up some beer to go? I was in the midst of my research on beer styles, so I hunted down several styles I had never tried before, including a brandywine and the original modern California common, Anchor Steam, and we made a customized six-pack of beers to enjoy while we brewed.

Monday, April 6: Brew Day

Brew day is the first of the two labor-intensive days in brewing a batch of beer, and it was actually a pretty nice way to liven up the typical Monday doldrums. Between brew day and bottling day, brew day is more involved, with more chances for things to go awry; that said, it's also the more exciting of the two days, too. (By the time you've finally capped the final bottle of your first home brew, you'll agree with me.)

Dut and I both got home from work around 5:30, and then we ran over to our local grocery store to grab 3 gallons of distilled water, the final ingredient we needed. (Our recipe was a partial boil, meaning that we would actually boil only around half of the full beer amount and then top off the end boil with distilled water to reach a total volume of 5 gallons.) After a quick dinner, we started the cleaning and sanitizing process at around 7:00.

Our grain bill for this pale ale was half a pound of crushed Crystal 20L malt and half a pound of crushed American 6-row malt for steeping and 5½ pounds of dry light malt extract for boiling. Unfortunately, Liquor Barn didn't have those crushed grains, but they did have the cracked variety, so we decided to just purchase the cracked grains and crush them at home. Because the nonextract grains were just for steeping, meaning that they would be used predominantly for flavor and color at the very beginning of the brewing process, they didn't need to be as finely crushed as the extract grains, which were a fine powder. (In fact, pulverizing the grains could even potentially inhibit a proper steeping.)

I read a really nice analogy during my initial home-brewing research that compared cracked grains to pistachios: to get at the nut meat in a pistachio (i.e., the good stuff), you need to crack it open, and the same is true with malted barley. In fact, cracked grains even resemble unshelled pistachios. The grain "meat" inside of the hull is the valuable ingredient for your beer, and the crushing process allows those grains to impart their colors and flavors to your grain tea.

After we sanitized the necessary equipment, I set about crushing up our steeping grains. Ideally, you would use a roller mill to do this (most brewing-supply stores have one, and they can either crush the grain for you or allow you to do it yourself for a small fee), but in *The Complete Joy of Homebrewing*, Charlie Papazian advises putting small amounts of grain in a zip-top bag and rolling over it with a rolling pin for a similar effect. Home brewing is nothing if not scrappy—at least for Mother Hen Brewing, anyway—so a-crushing I did go. It took a little while to crush a full pound of grains, but, all in all, I was pretty pleased with the results.

Crushed grains, ready for steeping.

Our recipe dictated raising 1 gallon of water to 160 degrees F and steeping the grains for 20 minutes. I got the water heating while Dut hooked up the wort chiller. (He was a little nervous about it working properly, so he wanted to get a head start on it; he tends to get a little stressed on brew days.) After the water hit 160 degrees, I put the crushed grains in the steeping bag, tied it to the handle of the brew kettle to keep it from falling in, and set a timer for 20 minutes.

After that initial steeping time, I returned the kettle to direct heat, raising the temperature up to 170 degrees F. I also tied the steeping bag of grains a little higher—it needed to be suspended off the bottom of the kettle to avoid direct heat because malted barley can give off unpleasant tannins if it gets too hot, resulting in —you guessed it—off-flavors. After the grain tea hit the target temperature, I pulled the steeping bag out and drained as much liquid from it as I could without squeezing it, which can lead to additional sediment in the beer and a cloudy appearance.

Keep It Clean

You've probably figured out by now that the cardinal rule of home brewing–in my book, anyway, though many home brewers would agree with me–is to clean and sanitize your equipment obsessively. Any remaining physical debris on your brewing equipment or in your bottles can completely ruin a batch of beer. The presence of greedy little microorganisms and bacteria can render an entire batch undrinkable with off-flavors and can even keep the yeast from properly doing its job. After you soak a piece of equipment in the sanitizing solution, it's important not to rinse it off, even though that may be your instinct. The cleaning solution residue does not affect the taste of flavor or your beer, and it will continue to help protect the equipment from bacteria.

The contents of your steeping bag can simply be thrown away, but they're also great to add to the compost pile, to feed to your livestock—poultry, pigs, and cattle love spent grains—and even to cook with. With a little additional work, spent grains make excellent granola, bread, cookies, and other baked goods. (Before you use them for human consumption, I recommend blitzing them in a food processor or blender with a little water to reduce the hull size.)

There was now only one step left before the boil: adding the extract. As I mentioned earlier, our recipe called for a partial boil, so we added enough water to bring our grain tea up to 3 gallons This water doesn't need to be distilled because the impurities in it will boil out over the course of wort creation, but it also doesn't hurt if you want to be extra cautious. As this diluted grain tea came up to boil, we added in the 5½ pounds of dry light malt extract little by little, stirring all the while. Since the malt extract is basically just a starch-based sweetener, the fumes coming off the brew pot became a little sticky, and our range-top hood needed a good scrubbing when all was said and done. (Boiling sugary wort for an hour will do that.)

Next, we kept the mixture over high heat until it was vigorously boiling. Unfortunately, our electric range took quite a while to do that—more than 20 minutes. Nonetheless, we soon had a chalky-colored but delicious-smelling prewort bubbling away, and once the boil began in earnest, we added half an ounce of Centennial hops and set a timer for 45 minutes. (The total boil time, like most recipes, was 60 minutes, but we needed to add more hops after 45 minutes of boiling.) The initial hops are known as the bittering hops, because the longer they boil, the more bitter they get; this helps counteract the syrupy-sweet taste your beer would have without any bittering agents at all.

When you remove the steeping bag, let the liquid drain out.

Hop pellets are recommended for beginning brewers.　　**Centennial hops in dried form.**

Because most recipes call for a weight of hops to be added to the boil, you can use either hop pellets or whole hops (also called leaf or raw hops) for your beer, but if you're a beginner, I'd strongly recommend sticking with pellets. Hop pellets are simply the whole hop flowers ground down and compressed into pellets, and they are significantly easier to use than their leafy companions—pellets are more stable, less likely to oxidize (read: smell cheesy and potentially ruin your beer), and easier to handle and clean up, whereas whole hops can soak up more wort, leaving you with less of a final product, and can also clog your siphon when you go to bottle your beer. That said, whole hops are the romantic choice for home brewers looking for the maximum DIY approach, but hop pellets are a great way to begin, and we used those in The Little Jerry.

Thankfully, the boil is relatively hands off—that's not to say that you can just walk out of the kitchen and leave a simmering pot on the stove, but you can sit back and relax with a beer while keeping an eye on your wort. (We tossed around name ideas for a while and then launched into a discussion of future styles we wanted to try.) The main objective is to keep the wort boiling vigorously for the entire hour.

After the 45-minute boil of our bittering hops, we added an ounce of Cascade hops and another ounce of Centennial to the mix for the final 15 minutes of boiling time—these are known as flavoring hops, because they impart a significant hop flavor to the final product without adding substantial bitterness. Because pale ales tend to be hoppy but not overly bitter, you'll notice that there were comparatively few bittering hops next to the flavoring ones. During these last 15 minutes of boiling, Dut checked (and rechecked) the wort chiller—not that I blame him. We had never used it before, and despite all of the reassurance from my research and our other home-brewing friends, the thought of putting a length of coiled copper tubing into our wort was still a little sobering because if we introduced bacteria at this stage, it could keep the beer from fermenting properly (or at all) or give it off-flavors. (Off-flavors are definitely a recurring theme in the realm of home-brew problems.)

Our final timer went off, and we added one more ounce of Cascade hops and another half-ounce of Centennial hops as we took the brew kettle off the heat. These were the last of the three hop additions, the aroma hops, and it's pretty easy to guess what these are for. Remember those volatile compounds that beer glasses are designed to capture? Some of them are given off by the hops, and these volatiles do not like steam and heat very much, so a final batch of hops is added at the very end of the boil to give pale ales that delectable hoppy aroma we all know and love.

Now it was time for the moment of truth: using the wort chiller for the first time. We sanitized the coil, immersed it in our hard-won wort, and turned on the faucet as cold as it would go. Because Mother Hen Brewing is a scrappy little operation, we just took turns holding a towel over the copper-plastic connections because we had a very slow leak. Even with that miniscule dripping, it only took 10 minutes to lower our wort to room temperature (70 degrees F), while our last batch, using our ice-bath method, took almost 45 minutes—the immersion chiller was definitely worth it. We were both more comfortable with the bacteria risk from the chiller than we were with the extended period of cooling time from an ice bath. The ice bath works, but the longer your beer sits before moving to its primary fermentor, the higher the chance of bacterial infection.

We got our wort to 70 degrees F, transferred it to our fermenting bucket, and then topped it off with a little more than 2 gallons of distilled water to bring the total liquid to 5 gallons. Unlike the water we added before the boil, this water has to be distilled; otherwise, we'd just be pouring potentially bacteria-ridden water into our wort. (Again, this step was necessary because we were doing a partial boil.)

There was only one final step before sealing the fermenting bucket and stashing it away in a cool, dark place: pitching the yeast. Our yeast strain did not need to be activated (i.e., mixed into warm water) to work, so we sanitized the outside of the package (you can never be too cautious, I'm telling you), sprinkled the yeast into our wort, and stirred vigorously with a sanitized spoon for 30 seconds (gotta get that yeast excited to start working on that sugar!). Safale US-05 yeast is rated to work between 59 and 75 degrees F, so it was imperative that we brought the wort into that temperature range before pitching the yeast.

If you'd like to know the final alcohol by volume (ABV) percentage for your batch of home brew, you'll need to take two gravity readings of the wort and beer—one on brew day and one on bottling day—

The wort chiller is submerged in the liquid and cools it via cold water running through its copper tubing.

and you'll also need several pieces of additional equipment: a hydrometer, a hydrometer container, and a wine thief. (Check out Chapter 4 for more information.) It's not necessary to know the ABV of your home-brewed batches, and you can brew delicious beer without ever truly thinking about the ABV, but at some point, you'll probably want to learn how to take the appropriate readings so you can answer your friends' questions about how strong your home brew is.

Thankfully, the process is quite easy. Make sure that your wine thief is properly sanitized and then use it to remove around ¾ cup of wort. You'll want to get this in one go, if possible, because additional dips into the wort are just additional chances to contaminate the batch. Empty the wort into your hydrometer container and drop the hydrometer inside with a spinning motion. The hydrometer will bob and float as it stabilizes, at which point you'll want to record the number where the wort line hits the hydrometer. This is your original gravity, which is a measurement of how much fermentable sugar your wort contains. (Water's specific gravity is 1.000,

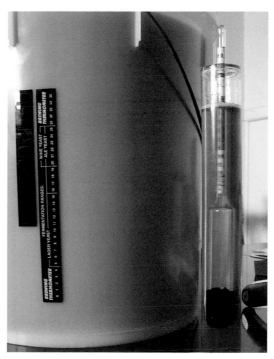

The hydrometer reading on this ale shows 1.042.

so the higher your measurement, which will usually be between 1.030 and 1.110, the more sugar your wort contains, which will likely mean a higher ABV in your end product). Make sure that you record this number, because if you don't, there's no going back to figure out the correct ABV of your final product! Our original gravity for The Little Jerry was 1.052, which we were pretty happy with.

We had our original gravity reading and the yeast was pitched successfully, so we snapped the lid on the bottling bucket, thinking that we had successfully brewed another batch of wort. Little did we know that we were in for five minutes of frantic stress and panic.

Dut added a little distilled water to the airlock, which would allow us to see the carbon dioxide produced by the fermenting process (the airlock has to be sanitized and the water in it has to be distilled). He then went to insert the pointy end into the rubber grommet that keeps the lid airtight. It was sticking a little bit, so he had to push pretty hard to get the narrow end into the grommeted hole. He was pushing and pushing when suddenly...pop! The piece of rubber that keeps the seal on the lid broke free of the plastic and splashed down into our wort. Cue panic. How were we going to create an anaerobic system for our wort to ferment in?

I'd like to say that we both keep cool heads in a crisis, but that would be a lie. Amid a flurry of vulgarities that I will not list here, we debated our options, and, fortunately, we had a few. Reaching in after the rubber grommet to pull it out was not ideal because our hands and arms are covered in bacteria, and the rubber did not seem to be floating, meaning that our chances for contamination would skyrocket if we had to reach all the way in and fish around for it. We also briefly considered transferring the wort into our glass carboy to ferment, but then we remembered that we had another grommeted lid because we have one fermenting bucket with a spigot and one without. There was momentary relief as we quickly swapped out lids, and Dut gingerly affixed the airlock into the grommeted hole. Talk about not knowing your own strength.

Original Gravity Reading

Some people advocate taking an original gravity reading before pitching the yeast, but the yeast doesn't have any major effects on the hydrometer reading because it's never going into solution with the wort–the yeast particles are only floating in the wort (i.e., in suspension), and hydrometers measure the gravity of a solution, not a suspension. The only major downside to taking a sample after you pitch the yeast is that the yeast particles in your sample will be removed from your batch while it ferments. (For safety's sake, it's best to dump your sample after you get a gravity reading; you risk contamination of your entire batch otherwise.) If you're concerned about the yeast waste, go ahead and take your sample before you pitch your yeast (we meant to, but unfortunately forgot!).

It was only after we had successfully sealed off the wort to ferment that we realized our secondary predicament—sure, we had created an anaerobic system for our fermenting wort, but that rubber grommet was going to just have to sit in our beer as it fermented, and neither of us had any idea if that little piece of rubber would have any ill effects on the fermentation process or the final taste of the beer. It had just been sanitized with the lid minutes earlier, so that part wasn't concerning, but would the rubber somehow stop the yeast from working properly or give the beer one of those dreaded off-flavors? Unfortunately, we had no way of knowing because my frantic Googling didn't produce any definitive results.

Resigned to our fate, we moved the fermenting bucket into a cool, dark closet—this was another time when we were happy about choosing to ferment in a bucket over a carboy for its easy portability. The location of your fermenting vessel doesn't matter too much, as long as the temperature stays constant and the container stays out of direct sunlight. The UV rays in natural light will cause skunky flavors in your beer when the light reacts with the hop oils, and fluctuating temperatures, like those near a heating and cooling vent, can mess with the yeast's effectiveness, so a closet is probably best.

We washed our equipment and finished our beers, happy that brew day had gone so well, but neither of us could shake that vague fear that GrommetGate had put a damper on The Little Jerry before it had truly begun.

Tuesday, April 7

Success (and massive sighs of partial relief!)! The airlock was bubbling away and the cool, dark closet where we were storing the beer had a pleasant hop aroma, as did that whole wing of the apartment—no one was complaining. I've never had a batch of beer fail to start fermenting properly, but I'd be lying if I didn't say that I usually spend the first 24 hours after brew day with bated breath until I see a few bubbles in the airlock, whether or not a rubber grommet is soaking in the batch of beer. Science, man.

The recipe we used recommended keeping the temperature of the wort between 62 and 66 degrees F; however, the recipe author also mentioned that he fermented his batch at 68 degrees and it turned out well, not to mention that most ales usually ferment at average room temperatures without any issues. In the end, we decided to ferment at 68 degrees F, mainly because the yeast strain we used—Safale US-

05—recommended a fermentation temperature between 59 and 75 degrees F for optimum results, and 68 degrees F was smack in the middle. Additionally, because we were brewing in spring in Kentucky, we knew that we would need to harness our heating and air conditioning to avoid massive indoor temperature fluctuations, which are definitely common, so we set our system to 68 degrees F for that week. That's definitely cooler than we like it inside for the beautiful mid-70s days that were forecasted for the week, but sometimes you have to make sacrifices for your home brew, you know?

Wednesday, April 8

The airlock was still bubbling away, but perhaps less intensely than we'd like. This is when I started to question our choice of fermenting in a bucket, because it would be great to see the yeast working. That said, it's not unheard of for an ale to complete primary fermentation in just a few days, especially with our specific yeast strain, so it was possible—and even likely—that this batch was nearing the end of its tenure in the fermenting bucket. (Either that, or our bucket wasn't airtight, and the carbon dioxide being produced was escaping somewhere else. We had double- and triple-checked the lid's seal, so I just chalked it up to worst-case-scenario thinking.)

Thursday, April 9

The bubbling in the airlock continued to slow down. We forgot to turn the air conditioner on before we left for work this morning, so when I came home in the evening, the fermentor was at 72 degrees F. Not a huge deal, but we gently cooled it back down to 68 degrees F as quickly as possible. Thankfully, 72 degrees F is still in the optimum range for our yeast strain to work; it would have been a concern if the temperature had risen (or dropped) outside of that range. Too high, and the yeast can produce higher numbers of fruity esters or other flavor compounds that can throw off the flavor of the end product; too low, and the yeast may not properly ferment at all, resulting in a slowed or even incomplete fermentation. This could even be erring on the side of caution, though, as some common strains of brewer's yeast have been proved to still work at temperatures as high as 110 degrees F— granted, the real question here is if the finished beer tasted like Hawaiian Punch or Juicy Fruit gum by the end. (Actually, that gives me a few brewing ideas…)

Saturday, April 11

No bubbles today at all—this is a good thing. Once we don't see any bubbles for 48 hours, we tend to go ahead and bottle. This is a good rule of thumb for ales; lagers tend to take longer due to the lower fermentation temperatures that they require. We've elected not to do a secondary fermentation for this batch, mainly because this style of beer doesn't require it to be properly flavored and, to be completely honest, we were eager to give the beer a try. The secondary fermentation would have clarified the beer, giving it a clearer appearance and likely a mellower, cleaner taste; this additional step benefits a good number of lagers and high-alcohol ales, such as barleywines and imperial stouts, but for a li'l ol' pale ale like ours, it's not necessary.

Monday, April 13

No bubbles again today, so we've decided to go ahead and bottle tomorrow. Also, it's a good thing that we went ahead and manually kept the temperature constant because during the week of fermentation, temperatures dipped into the upper 30s at night and climbed into the low 80s during the hottest parts of the week. Welcome to springtime in Kentucky!

Tonight, we decided to get a head start on the bottling-day activities and start removing the labels from our saved beer bottles. By this point, you know that Mother Hen Brewing is an operation that likes to save money wherever possible, so we'd been saving beer bottles for most of 2015 in order to have the required fifty by bottling day.

Removing the existing labels on beer bottles is pretty simple, if a bit time-consuming. Basically, you just need to soften the adhesive on the bottles by soaking them in hot water for an hour or so, and then you peel what you can of the labels off and scrub the rest off with a stiff brush, sponge, or scouring pad. We soaked the bottles before dinner and then, after dinner, we set up an assembly line in the kitchen sink, scrubbing and scratching until our bottles shined. It's not the quickest process—it took us an hour or so to scrub fifty bottles—but it is definitely cathartic and somewhat of a stress reliever.

In this step, we're not cleaning the inside of the bottles at all, choosing to do that on bottling day proper. Similar to chilling wort, the longer clean bottles sit open to the air, the greater the chance of them getting infected with some kind of bacteria. So we set the label-free bottles up to dry on the kitchen counter until the next night.

Now, you don't actually have to put your beer into single-serving bottles to carbonate; you can also choose to put the beer into a kegging system where you force-carbonate the beer with carbon dioxide, which saves you a little time in waiting for the beer to be drinkable after fermentation, which is a definite plus. The downside is the cost of equipment because purchasing a kegging setup can usually be a pretty large investment—sometimes as much as several hundred dollars—in comparison to the rest of the ingredients and equipment.

Soaking the bottles helps label removal go faster.

As I've mentioned, Dut and I like to keep our costs down as much as we can, so we've never invested in a kegging setup. Many experts will tell you that once you keg a batch of home brew, you'll never go back to bottling, and I'll be the first to admit that bottling beer is not nearly as enjoyable as brewing it. However, that cost hurdle, plus the additional equipment we would need to store in our relatively small apartment, has kept us from taking the plunge. We also tend to give a good portion of our beer away to friends and family, and constantly filling up from a keg-attached beer wand is more time-consuming than just grabbing a few bottles to take to a party. That's not to say that we won't ever keg a batch, but with our casual home-brewing schedule, bottling has served us well so far.

Tuesday, April 14:

Bottling Day

Bottling day has arrived! It's the last real day of any actual work with the beer. The only thing left to do after bottling is just wait for the beer to carbonate, which is maybe the most difficult stretch of time in the home-brewing process—there's nothing like filling fifty bottles with beer and then being forced to wait while they carbonate slowly over a week or two, taunting you with their mere presence.

Sanitized bottles, ready to be filled.

We started the evening off by mixing up a batch of sanitizing solution in the brew kettle instead of in our other fermenting bucket, which is where we normally keep the sanitizer, because we would soon be siphoning the beer from our spigotless fermenting vessel into the brew bucket with the spigot. As with brew day, proper sanitization is key to a delicious final product, and proper attention now will save you headaches and disappointment later. After we got that started, we filled a small mixing bowl with some of the solution and dropped fifty bottle caps into it to sanitize them—you certainly don't want to seal your hard-earned beer with a bacteria-laden cap and ruin the bottles one by one!

Some people recommend using cheap vodka to sanitize the caps because caps that have been soaked in normal sanitizing solution tend to rust if they're not used immediately, but we always count out an exact number of caps, so rusting isn't a major issue for us. That said, if you buy a bulk bag of bottle caps like we did, I would refrain from putting all of them into the sanitizing solution. Sanitize only as many as you'll need and save the rest for your next batch. Vodka does work just as well, and the caps won't rust if you soak them all, but when you have sanitizing solution already made for your other equipment, it only makes sense to me to use some for the bottle caps, too.

Once the caps were soaking, we started the cleaning assembly line. But was the cleaner, and I was the sanitizer: we filled up one side of our sink with hot water and OxiClean for the scrubbing and cleaned the insides of the bottles with a bottling brush. After a vigorous rinsing, I soaked the bottles for at least a full minute in the sanitizing solution before pulling them out and setting them on the prongs of our bottling tree, which we had sanitized before starting to clean the bottles.

Most people will tell you that a bottling tree is an unnecessary piece of equipment because you can just set the bottles on a sanitized surface to dry after you've finished cleaning them and before you fill them, but I'd encourage you to invest in one—Northern Brewer Homebrew Supply (**www.northernbrewer.com**) sells a model that unscrews for easy storage and allows you to hang forty-five bottles to dry. A bottling tree helps minimize your chances for contamination between cleaning and filling and allows you some added peace of mind while you bottle your beer. Just make sure to sanitize it first before you start placing bottles on the prongs.

Anyway, an hour or so later, we had fifty cleaned and sanitized bottles just waiting to be filled with The Little Jerry. Next on the docket was to sanitize the equipment we'd be using: the siphon, bottling wand, and hose—both inside and out—plus the bottling bucket, remembering to run sanitizing solution through the spigot itself. While Dut took care of sanitizing those pieces, I mixed our priming sugar—4.5 ounces of corn sugar—with 2 cups of tap water and set the solution to boil.

There are a number of ways to carbonate your beer, but we've always used the priming-sugar method: mix a basic simple syrup into your beer before you bottle it, and the yeast in each bottle will act on that sugar over a number of days or weeks, creating carbon dioxide, which is trapped in the bottle until you crack it open. (This is the same basic process as the beer's primary fermentation, but the produced carbon dioxide there can escape through the airlock, which allows gas to escape without introducing more to the wort.) Some brewers prefer adding sugar or sugar syrup to each individual bottle, but that seems time-consuming and full of unnecessary effort, so we always just mix the sugar syrup into the beer after we siphon it into the bottling bucket, and we've yet to have any issues.

The recipe we used called for 10 minutes of boiling the sugar with the water, which I had never heard of before; normally, we just bring the syrup to a boil and let it cool a bit before adding it—but this time we boiled for the full 10 minutes, choosing to follow the recipe and trust the author. (That's a pretty solid rule to live by when brewing beer, especially in your early batches.)

While I kept an eye on the boiling syrup, Dut primed the siphon by running tap water through it until all the air was out of the hose. Clamping it shut, he placed the end of it into the sanitizing solution and unclamped it until all the tap water was replaced with sanitizer, clamping the end shut again once that happened. Last but not least, he placed the racking cane into the bucket, clipping it to the side and sinking the end into the beer. After unclamping the other end, he ran the sanitizing solution into a bowl until the first spurts of beer began to come out, at which point he moved the end into the sanitized bottling bucket and started to siphon the beer proper. (You can just toss the sanitizing solution in the bowl down the drain.)

Siphoning is usually a pretty painless process once it begins—the biggest thing to worry about is keeping the nozzle of the racking cane submerged in the beer the entire time. If the end is exposed to air, the suction in the siphon will stop, and you'll need to repeat the process at the beginning of this step all over again. (Not a huge deal, but annoying nonetheless.) You'll also need to leave between a half-inch and an inch of beer in the fermenting vessel; this final amount at the bottom of the barrel is packed with hop sediment, and you don't particularly want to clog your racking cane with that sludge. Plus, hop sediment in a bottle of beer isn't

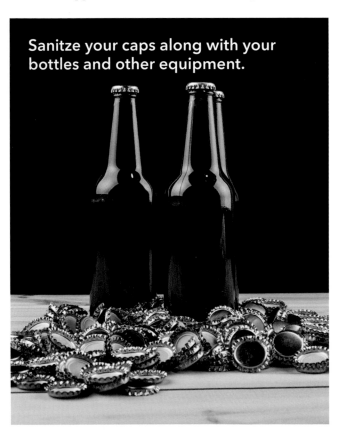

Sanitze your caps along with your bottles and other equipment.

exactly desirable to the palate, either: it can taste chalky and bitter, souring the final sip of a bottle.

We erred on the side of caution here, leaving a little more beer behind than we could have, but we were also vaguely still concerned about that rubber grommet getting sucked up into the siphon and stopping the flow. After stopping the suction flow, we went ahead and took our final gravity reading. The process is the same as taking the original gravity reading: sanitize your wine thief, take around ¾ cup of beer from the bottling bucket, and empty the beer into the hydrometer container. Drop your hydrometer into the sample with a spinning motion and record the number at the beer level once the hydrometer stabilizes. Again, you shouldn't pour your sample back into your bottling bucket, but you can save this uncarbonated beer to get an idea of how your final product will taste.

To figure out the ABV of your beer, take your original gravity measurement and subtract your final gravity from it. Once you have a decimal, multiply it by 131 to get your ABV percentage. Our final gravity for The Little Jerry

If you keep the nozzle of the racking cane submerged, you should have no trouble siphoning.

was 1.011, which gave us a decimal of 0.041 when subtracted from our original gravity, 1.052. Multiplying that by 131 gave us an ABV of 5.371%, which is right in the middle of the average pale-ale ABV range—good by us! I must mention that this formula is an approximation of the ABV value for a beer, and it's usually within half a percentage point of the actual value. For more information, head over to **www. homebrewdad.com/abv_calculator.php**.

After calculating our ABV, I gently mixed the priming-sugar syrup into the beer, making sure to scrape the bottom and stir all parts of the bucket to properly incorporate it. Once it was all stirred in, we placed the lid over the bottling bucket to keep the open air from touching the beer while we bottled as much as possible.

Two more major steps to bottling day: filling the bottles and sealing the bottles. Now, I must admit, of all the myriad equipment used in the beer-brewing process, my favorite gizmo has to be the bottling wand. This ingenious device hooks onto the spigot of your bottling bucket and allows you to fill your bottles with no wasted beer and with minimal time and effort. Basically, it consists of just a clear plastic tube with a spring-loaded tip. You hook the nontipped end over the spigot of your bottling bucket and open the tap, causing the tube to fill with beer. You then place the tube inside a bottle, pressing the tip against the bottom of the bottle, which opens the spring-loaded tip and fills the bottle with beer. Once the liquid level reaches the bottle's rim, pull the bottle down to shut off the flow and then remove the bottle from the tube. The liquid level will decrease as the tube exits the bottle, leaving you with between ½ and 1 inch of headspace for the beer to carbonate. In 15 seconds or so, you've successfully filled a bottle with beer without wasting a drop, and you've also kept the entire process sanitary. Given the fact that bottling wands usually cost between two and three dollars, you can't ask for much more than that.

The bottling and capping process is easiest with two people: one to fill bottles and one to affix the airtight caps on them. You can definitely manage it with one person, but expect to spend roughly double

the time finishing the steps (obviously). With two people, you just create an assembly line in which the filler fills a bottle and passes it to the capper, who takes a sanitized cap out of the bowl that you set aside earlier—remember that?—and attaches it to the bottle's neck with a capper. If you'll be flying solo for this process, you can either fill each bottle and immediately cap it or place a sanitized cap on the neck of each bottle but wait to seal the caps until you've filled all your bottles. The latter option will expedite the process as much as possible while still keeping everything safe and sanitary.

For this batch, Dut opted to fill while I capped. We use a wing capper, which has two handles that you depress to create the bottle's seal. Bench cappers are a popular alternative because they're easier to use, but they are also more expensive. (It's not surprising to see that we chose the wing capper.)

The whole affair took about half an hour without any mishaps—the only bump in the road was realizing that we had accidentally saved a few twist-off bottles in our bottle-saving endeavor. The problem with reusing twist-off bottles for home brewing is that the grooves that allow the cap to be easily removed don't offer much space for a non-twist-off cap to attach itself to the bottle neck, meaning that even if you get a seemingly tight seal, it's usually just a matter of time until the seal breaks and that bottle spoils, either through oxygenation or decarbonation. Some home brewers report having no issues with reusing twist-off bottles, but it's probably best to play it safe and save only pry-off bottles. Anyway, we had saved only three or four twist-off bottles by accident, so we just didn't use those. We did fill one by mistake, discovering that it was a twist-off bottle only after I couldn't get the capper to create a proper seal, so we just carefully transferred that beer into another usable bottle.

In the end, we had forty-six longneck bottles and one bomber of The Little Jerry ready for the carbonation waiting period. We could have probably gotten another bottle or so out of the fermenting bucket, but, again, because of that rubber grommet, we decided to just leave it. After all of my research, I didn't think that the grommet would be detectable in the final taste of the beer, and it clearly hadn't affected fermentation, so it seemed that GrommetGate wouldn't have any lasting impact on our beer. Just to be sure, though, we saved the sample from our final gravity reading to taste.

Before diving in, though, we moved all of the bottles onto a shelf in the same closet where we fermented the wort—the most important condition for successful carbonation is letting the bottles sit at room temperature. Don't be tempted to move a few bottles into the fridge in preparation because the cool temperatures will cause the yeast to go into hibernation and stop acting on the sugar; in the same vein, don't place the bottles in a room where the temperature rises and falls frequently, such as the kitchen. If you use your oven frequently, those temperature fluctuations can mess up the yeast's final job.

After a toast to a successful bottling day and an exchange of slightly worried grimaces, Dut and I took our first sips of The Little Jerry, and you know what? It wasn't half bad. It had a very nice hoppiness up front, both in aroma and flavor, and was actually a touch sweeter than we were expecting it to be. The

Cascade hops lent the beer a pleasant citrus aftertaste, and the hops lingered long enough on the tongue to be enjoyed without overstaying their welcome. After the underlying worry we had been feeling for the past week, I think we were both surprised that the beer was not only drinkable, but actually seemed as if it were going to be quite enjoyable.

This brings up another point about home brewing that I've heard time and time again: beer recipes can be pretty forgiving. Even if your end result isn't exactly like the recipe specified it would be, it's more than likely still going to be a delicious, drinkable brew, provided that you sanitized religiously and followed protocol. And that's half the fun of home brewing to me—each batch is unique and usually comes with a story to tell your friends and family when you share a bottle with them. (You better believe that GrommetGate is going to be discussed in detail over the next several weeks.)

A spoiled batch is another story entirely, I suppose, but the fleeting transience of home-brewed beer is part of the magic behind it, I think. That beer is almost guaranteed to taste delicious because you took the time and put in the effort to make it yourself. That's how I felt about those first sips of this pale ale, anyway.

As we cleaned and dried our equipment and put everything away, neither Dut nor I could really wipe the smiles off our faces. A successfully brewed and bottled batch of beer will do that to you, I guess.

Wednesday, April 15

No exploded bottles…yet. Here's hoping it stays that way! We've never had a bottle explode, and I'd like to keep it that way. Granted, we've never brewed a heavily carbonated beer, either, so that could eventually change in the future, but because pale ales are about middle of the road in carbonation level, we're not really expecting any issues with these bottles.

A wing capper gets the job done on a budget.

Tuesday, April 21

Bottles still look good! The beer was potentially drinkable today, but leaving the bottles to carbonate for another week at room temperature will take the beer to its best levels of carbonation. Although I like some low-carbonation beer styles, a pale ale is not one of them, so I'm all about waiting another week to try the first Little Jerry (no matter how hard it may be to wait…sigh).

Saturday, April 25

Still no exploded bottles. T-minus three days until we break open the first bottle of this batch.

Monday, April 27

We had our final naming discussion today, and we decided for certain to call this beer The Little Jerry pale ale. I can feel your collective eyebrow-raising that's been going on since the beginning of this chapter, so let me explain.

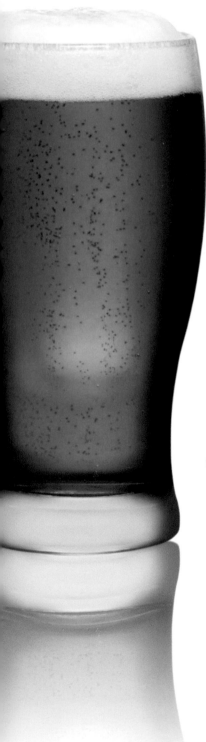

First of all, we wanted to tie this specific beer name back into our brewery name because we had yet to produce a chicken-themed beer and that seemed a disgrace to Mother Hen Brewing. Second, in our spare time, we had recently finished a grand rewatch of all nine seasons of *Seinfeld*, Dut's favorite TV show and one of my top three, so it felt appropriate to tip our collective hat to such an iconic piece of entertainment, especially since we recently had been saturated with it. And so we tried to find a bridge between chickens and Seinfeld—it didn't take us very long.

In the eighth season, there's an episode called "The Little Jerry" in which Kramer finds himself upset with the droopy and flavorless "sweatshop eggs" in his diner breakfast, so he decides to take matters into his own hands by purchasing a chicken of his very own for cage-free, farm-fresh eggs every morning. There's only one (admittedly major) problem: Kramer's chicken, which he has named Little Jerry Seinfeld in honor of his friend and neighbor, is a rooster, not a hen. Whoops. In typical Seinfeld fashion, wackiness ensues, and Kramer and Jerry find themselves training Little Jerry for an illegal cockfight, which ends with Kramer diving into the ring to save Little Jerry from his formidable opponent, described as "a dog with a glove on his head." The episode is hysterical, with multiple bits of physical comedy featuring Kramer and Little Jerry: walking the rooster on a makeshift leash, checking its rump for eggs, and grabbing the bird upside down after it attacks a dog.

To be honest, the beer basically named itself.

We particularly liked the somewhat obscure reference to chickens in the title—I know it's a stretch to call one of the highest-rated sitcoms of all time "obscure," but you have to admit that it's less obvious than the Foghorn Leghorn pale ale (not that we ever considered that name)—and the tongue-in-cheekiness of the moniker. Plus, it didn't hurt that Little Jerry the rooster was orangish-brown in color, which was not too far off from the orange-leaning projected color of the pale ale recipe we used.

Anyway, unlike some of our past home brews, there was next to no debate on this name. We both liked it basically right off the bat, and it just felt right from the moment Dut suggested it.

Only one final step in The Little Jerry saga: tomorrow's tasting.

Tuesday, April 28

Finally, it's tasting day! It has been six weeks in the making since we first starting discussing brewing another batch of beer; granted, only three of those weeks involved the actual brewing process, but it still seems like a very long time when you have to wait.

When I got home from work, I popped two Little Jerrys into the fridge to chill while I made dinner. After the dishes were washed, we just couldn't wait any longer, and I pulled out the chilled bottles and two pint glasses. (N.B.: When you're drinking beer, especially when you're taking the first taste of a batch, don't use chilled glasses. Glasses kept in the freezer tend to take on the flavors of the foods they're stored with, so stick to well-cleaned, room-temperature glasses for the best tasting experience.)

Popping the caps off the bottles created a satisfying hiss—our carbonation had definitely worked! The smell out of the bottleneck was decidedly hop-forward with some nice citrus undertones, and pouring the beer into the glasses produced a thick, foamy, white head on the top of the pleasantly cloudy, pale-orangish beer. The color leaned a little toward the amber side of things, but that was what we expected from the recipe because the steeping grains and the malt extract were both a little deeper in color than most pale ales require. The head stuck around for a while, too, which was a nice surprise. Pale ales aren't exactly known for their head retention, but that white foam kept those volatile compounds from the Cascade and Centennial hops lingering around for most of the glass.

Two chilled Little Jerrys, nicely carbonated and pale amber in color.

As far as taste itself was concerned, The Little Jerry presented itself as an eminently drinkable brew—it was smooth, with a creamy mouthfeel, and really nicely balanced. There was definitely a malty sweetness there, but it was quickly countered by the hops' citrusy bitterness. The hops were most prevalent in the first part of the sip, and, as you swallowed, the underlying sweetness prevailed for a nice, calm aftertaste. The malty flavor had some caramel notes that paired really nicely with the orangey hops. The beer was nicely carbonated, too, staying light and refreshing without straying into crazy Belgian levels of bubbles.

If anything, we would have dialed down the sweetness from the malt and upped the level of bittering hops slightly. Because we used only half an ounce of bittering hops and 3.5 ounces of aroma and flavoring hops, the beer had a strong hoppy character, but not the associated bitterness that tends to come along with it. We weren't setting out to make an IPA or anything, but maybe a full ounce of hops up front may have been a slightly better balance—but that's a minor complaint.

Honestly, we both thought that this was the best batch we've made yet: the process went exceedingly smoothly—save the GrommetGate adventure—and the resulting beer was pleasantly complex yet drinkable. We were legitimately quite excited to start passing this around our friend circles, and it goes without saying that we were pretty pleased with ourselves. There's no feeling quite like that first delicious sip of a successful home brew: you positively swell with pride. My only major regret is that I hadn't chilled two more Little Jerrys for a second tasting.

9

Small-Batch Brewing

Most home-brewing guides, this one included, recommend that you start with 5-gallon batches of beer. Five gallons is the standard across the board, and most home-brew supply stores sell equipment and ingredients that are presized for these batches for simplicity's sake. However, just because 5-gallon batches are the norm doesn't make them the only option. You can size down your batches to 1 or 2 gallons, which makes the whole process a bit more manageable, especially since the average home brewer isn't going to be drinking fifty 12-ounce bottles of beer (the average yield of a 5-gallon batch) all that quickly. A 1-gallon batch will give you ten bottles of beer, which you can store easily in your fridge or pantry. Let's look at the major benefits of shrinking your batch size.

HOPS SPRING WATER MALT

Lower Ingredient Costs

Home-brewing ingredient costs aren't terribly high to begin with, but you can cut those costs by more than half by making smaller batches, and this is particularly useful if you'd like to make a batch with higher-cost ingredients, like honey. Yeast will likely be the most expensive of your materials, but if you choose to use liquid yeast, you'll only use a quarter to half of the tube, so you'll have some additional yeast for future batches.

If you can find a home-brewing supply store that sells small quantities of grains and extracts, that's great, but don't despair if you have to buy a 3-pound bag of dry malt extract and you need only a fraction of it. Just store what's left in an airtight container and keep it at room temperature until you brew your next batch—crushed grains and dry malt extract will keep for two or three months like this, and uncrushed grains can last for up to a year. Hops, both pellet and whole-flower variety, are a little more finicky, though: they need to be protected from heat, light, and oxygen, so your best bet is storing them in your freezer in an airtight, light-safe plastic bag. Just make sure that they're not freezer-burned when you go to use them! Yeast is a no-brainer to store: keep it in the refrigerator until you're ready for it, and throw it away if it's past the expiration date on the package.

Smaller Storage Footprint

Here's the thing: 5-gallon buckets, carboys, and brew kettles are massive, and they take up a considerable amount of room, whether they're actively being used or just in storage. If you have a garage or an attic, it's pretty easy to store them out of the way, but if you're in a small apartment, you may not have that luxury. Smaller versions of those large pieces of equipment, though, are quite manageable—you can probably store most of your equipment under your bed. Plus, when you're bottle-conditioning a batch of beer, you can fit ten bottles into a much smaller space than fifty.

On the other hand, though, you'll need to spend a little money up front to purchase these smaller pieces of equipment; namely, a smaller fermenting vessel and brew kettle. In fact, if you have an 8- or 12-quart stockpot, that can double as your brew kettle as long as you wash it thoroughly before and after use. Most of your equipment for a 5-gallon batch can still be used for smaller batches, but you won't need the bottling wand and separate bottling bucket because you'll just be siphoning directly from your fermentor into your bottles.

Faster Brewing and Bottling Time

A smaller batch won't save you time in every single step—you'll still need to boil your wort for an hour, for instance—but you'll find that it takes significantly less time to bring your wort up to boil and to chill

Smaller batches mean smaller equipment.

it, too. In fact, a wort chiller is potentially rendered useless if you're cooling only one-fifth of the volume that you normally would have with a 5-gallon batch. Not only will your brew kettle easily fit into your sink, but the ice-bath method will work much faster. Plus, a wort chiller designed for a 5-gallon brew kettle likely won't even fit into your downsized pot. If you're brewing a small batch in your full-sized brew kettle, only a very small portion of the wort chiller's coils will even touch the hot wort.

The time you'll spend on bottling day is chopped considerably, too, because you'll be filling only ten bottles instead of fifty.

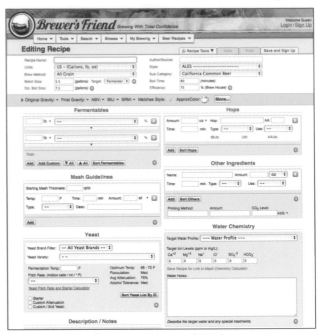

Recipe calculator from www.brewersfriend.com

Flying Solo

Brewing a 5-gallon batch of beer by yourself isn't the easiest thing, especially if you're using a glass carboy—those things are heavy when they're full of wort! In fact, I'd strongly recommend that you have someone around to help out on brew day and bottling day for a 5-gallon batch. A 1-gallon batch, though, is very manageable by yourself. If you live alone or you can't find someone who's willing to help out in the kitchen for a few hours, small-batch brewing can allow you to take charge of the process in a totally new way.

Jalapeno? Peppermint? You'll never know what will (or won't!) work until you try.

Go ahead and try those combinations you've been dreaming up!

Experimentation

Do you have an insatiable craving to try making a unique flavor combination, like a jalapeno stout or maybe a peppermint IPA? Here's where small batches are an excellent idea. Like any recipe experimentation, there's always a chance that these crazy-flavored beers will be terrible—but how are you going to know unless you try? If peppermint and hops turn out to be a less-than-appealing combo, you only have ten bottles to suffer through/dispose of; if they wind up being a match made in heaven, you can use one of the recipe calculators in the Resources section to size up your creation and start producing it on a larger scale.

In the end, it's up to you whether or not you want to shrink the size of your batches. There are definite up sides, but, in the same vein, your yield drops by 80 percent from a 5-gallon to a 1-gallon batch, and you'll need to home brew more frequently to keep your fridge stocked. (Is more frequent home brewing a bad thing, though? I'd say no.)

If you do decide to downsize, don't be so quick to get rid of your larger sized equipment—you may still want to return to 5-gallon batches at some point in the future, and you don't want to have to reinvest in a new brew kettle and carboy.

Branding

You've made you first batch of home brew, and now you've got two weeks to kill before you can break open the first bottle and have that inaugural taste. Why not spend some of that time brainstorming some fun and creative names for your beer and coming up with a great label design?

You certainly don't have to take these final steps in branding your home brew, but isn't that part the fun? You've created this (theoretically) delicious brew, so take it to the next level by tacking on a name that is worthy of your time and effort. Labeling your beers is definitely an advanced step, but if you're crafty at all, you may as well put those skills to use here, too—you can make your home brew a one-stop shop of delicious flavor and exciting, eye-catching design all in one. It's not nearly as exciting to give someone a painstakingly crafted smoked porter in a Sierra Nevada bottle with the label still attached. (Nothing against Sierra Nevada, of course, but you'd rather have your own label on that Hoppy Days IPA you brewed, no?)

The possibilities are endless, and the craft beer world is rife with puns, the king of which is potentially Ruckus Brewing's Hoptimus Prime, a double IPA that touches on two very powerful marketing strategies: nostalgia and humor. Be honest: even if you don't like IPAs, you're probably thinking about seeking out a six-pack of Hoptimus Prime next time you go to the liquor store because you just loved watching *Transformers* as a kid, and those Shia LaBoeuf movies weren't half bad, either.

Now, I'm certainly not advocating that you need to think like a professional marketing company for your first batch of home-brewed beer, but a creative name will go a long way among your family and friends. You'll be able to swell with pride when you get compliments on your home brew's whole package, not to mention the fact that a name and label design help you cement ownership of the beer you made.

There are three major levels to beer branding: brewery name, batch name, and logo/label design.

Naming Your Brewery

You'll probably want to name your brewery, especially if you plan to make multiple batches of beer. And don't blanch at calling your operation a "brewery," either: you've made a batch of beer, and beer is made only in breweries, so by the trusty old transitive property we all learned in elementary school, you are the operator of a brewery, no matter how small or new it may be. Feel free to qualify it with "home brewery" or something akin to that if you'd prefer, but for all intents and purposes, you're running a brewery. (Congratulations!)

To name your operation, the sky's the limit—you can pursue a number of naming avenues, including local geography, beer puns, and inside jokes, although I'll warn you right now that the market on the first two options is pretty crowded. Chances are, if you live in a city of decent size, there are already a number of locally named breweries with your city's name or local landmarks in the title. Plus, if you can think of any pun on beer's common ingredients, chances are also likely that someone else thought of it first. That said, obscure puns are certainly not unwelcome, either.

The worlds of home brewing and craft beer are deep, deep rabbit holes, so set your home brewery apart however you can. Do you have a defining characteristic that people always associate with you, like wearing red lipstick or adding the word "dude" to the end of every sentence? Try riffing on that for your brewery name to add an extra level of connection: Red Lipped Brewing or Whoa Dude Brewery could even become synonymous with you, if you home brew long enough. Or maybe you want to pay homage to a piece of entertainment that you're particularly fond of—think Winterfell Brewery or Lord of Light Brewing if you're a *Game of Thrones* fan, or maybe Thornfield Brewing or Red Room Brewery for those Victorian literature buffs among us (imagine it, *Jane Eyre* fans: the Madwoman in the Attic IPA!). Favorite sports teams, pets, geographical locations…the possibilities are basically endless, so go with whatever excites you most. If you do select a commercial property, however, it goes without saying that you cannot sell your beers for fear of copyright infringement.

If you always brew with a friend or group of friends, consider naming your operation after an inside joke or a common passion or goal that the group of you share. This is the strategy I took when my roommate and lifelong friend Dustin and I started to home brew. We have a long-standing history of chicken-related jokes, and, by this point, I can't even tell you how the whole chain of things began. What I do know is that a few years ago, in a late-night burst of creativity (read: procrastination) while I was in graduate school, I wrote a few chicken-themed folk songs, and the one that really stuck was called "Mother Hen." Sample lyric: "Oh, Mother Hen, she knows who's the boss of the chicken coop. (It's her, it's her.)" What can I say? Anyway, the song was a "hit" among my friends, so it was a natural choice for our brewery name. Dut and I loved the idea of a smug mother hen doling out home brew to the other farm animals, and Mother Hen Brewing was born.

Picking a themed name for your home-brewing operation can help inform your beer names in the future, too. Let's say you went with Winterfell Brewing as a *Game of Thrones* fan: your GoT references are basically endless. Winter Is Coming Oktoberfest, Dream of Spring Winter Warmer, Lannister's Golden Ale…the list goes on. You can name your home brews after characters, locations, and concepts from the vast world of Westeros and drive home the brewery name connection at the same time. Fair warning, though: if you're sharing your creations with nonfans, expect to do a considerable amount of explaining when you give them a bottle of that perfectly crafted homage to Daenerys Targaryen (Fire and Blood Red Ale? Sorry, I'll stop now.)

Start with a blank label and get creative.

At the very least, labels on your bottles will eliminate any confusion over what you're about to drink!

Naming Your Beers

Like I just mentioned, having a brewery name in place is a great starting point for future batch names, but your home brews' names don't have to be connected to your operation's name. I'll be the first to admit that a samey-samey naming strategy can be a bit cloying if it's laid on too thick. (Mother Hen Brewing has only put out one beer with a chicken-themed name, and it was the The Little Jerry pale ale that's detailed in Chapter 8.)

Let your imagination run wild when you're brainstorming beer names because there are no limits on what you can name your creations. As mentioned, the American craft-beer scene is quite partial to puns and jokes wherever possible, so that's always a nice place to start. You can riff on ingredient names—"hops" is probably the easiest and most common—or on the style that you're making. Let's say that you're brewing a witbier that toes the line with a little less wheat content than its brethren: try calling it Half-Wit or Dim Wit witbier.

Was there an event that took place during the brewing or bottling process that was noteworthy? You could spin that into a beer name—just try to keep the name positive if you can. I can't imagine that a lot of people will be thrilled about taking a swig of an Overboiled Amber Ale or a Temp Is Too Damn High Pale Ale. (Actually, I take that back—I'd try both of those. But stay away from the Possible Contamination Dunkel.)

Or maybe you were binge-watching a show on Netflix around the time you were brewing and bottling—take that idea for spin. Mother Hen Brewing's porter was named because we were playing through a classic video game of our childhoods, *The Legend of Zelda: Ocarina of Time,* for nostalgia's sake while we were brewing it. The dark, robust beer took its name from a dark and spooky character in the game: Skull Kid Porter. (Between that name and the names I brainstormed for Winterfell Brewing, I'm very clearly outing myself as a nerd here.)

You could even go the super-simple route and just name the beer after yourself: the John Doe Stout or the Jane Doe Cream Ale. Like I said, you don't have to think like a marketing professional: just name the beer whatever makes the most sense to you.

Label Design

This is the advanced step of beer branding, and it's definitely one you can skip if you're feeling overwhelmed. Unlike naming your operation and your creations, it requires additional supplies and potentially a large time investment. That said, you'll positively beam with pride when you see your loved ones tipping back a bottle of beer of which you created every single part (except the bottle, but maybe your next venture could be taking up glassblowing?).

You have a few options when it comes to creating your labels: you can purchase full sheets of blank, printable sticker or label paper and cut them into shape with scissors or an X-Acto knife; you can opt for pre-cut and pre-sized blank printable labels; or you can use an online service to design, print, and ship your labels. These options increase in cost one to the next. Buying full-sized blank sticker paper is pretty inexpensive, but you can expect to spend up to a dollar per label for labels that you design and print through a company; in this case, you may wind up spending more on your labels than on your ingredients.

Think outside the box for your presentation, too. What if labels aren't your style? Just grab a light-colored permanent marker or oil-based paint pen and draw on your bottles to your heart's content. You can customize each bottle identically or make each one unique. For the ultra-low-level DIYer, you can even just write the pertinent information on the bottle: beer name, brewery name, and ABV. (This is the category into which I fall. I'm not a particularly crafty person, but I do love the idea of personalizing each bottle and taking ownership as much as possible.)

If you're going the full-label route, don't forget to consider a logo for your beer as well. This can be as simple or complex as you like. You could design a geometrical abstract image, use a photo of your beer's or brewery's namesake, or even just go the font route and keep your labels simple. The logo is probably the least essential of these branding ideas, but it's still a great idea for a little added fun.

Again, these branding steps are all optional, and you can create an endlessly quaffable IPA without naming it at all, but I urge you to consider a name and label design. It's the satisfying cherry on top of the home-brewing sundae.

Home-brewed beer and homemade labels for Backpackers' Lager.

Troubleshooting

A plethora of things can go wrong when you're making your first batches of beer. Like so many other hobbies, home brewing is a learning process, but take comfort in the fact that you will continue to gain knowledge and refine your skill set the more you experiment with the process.

"The same problems can occur whether you've been brewing for two years or ten," says Colby Burke, a home brewer in Fort Collins, Colorado. He's learned a lot in two years, and now that he produces more consistent and enjoyable brews, he has his sights set on entering a home-brewing competition. "Beginners often don't follow exactly what they should, and it all comes down to note-taking," he adds.

Don't forget the importance of taking notes!

Record-keeping is one of the most important tools for every home brewer. Keeping logs of sanitation practices, equipment, recipes, ingredients, times, fermentation temperatures, room temperatures, and original and final gravity readings is the only way to ensure that you can fix problems when they arise and recreate a consistently good beer.

Most of the problems experienced by home brewers have simple solutions, but it takes some patience and knowledge to persevere. If you take good notes through every step of the process, then you can successfully tackle the common home-brewing problems that stand between you and the perfect pint.

This chapter is here to help you nail down home-brewing best practices and find answers to questions that you may have about issues with your batches, such as off-flavors or a lack of proper carbonation, and how to rectify them for future batches.

Common Glitches
Sanitation Issues

"Sanitation is key to good beer [that is] free from infection," says Chad Casper, a member of the Marin Society of Homebrewers in California and the winner of several home-brewing awards at the local, state, and national levels. You've heard it throughout this book, and both Casper and Burke agree: sanitation is arguably the most critical step in the home-brewing process, and it's the part that can most easily trip up a beginning home brewer. Although cleaning can remove dirt and residue, only sanitizing will kill the bacteria and reduce the presence of contaminants that can ruin a batch.

Anything that comes into contact with the wort or beer at any time after the boil should be sanitized. Pay special attention to hoses because cracks in the interior can trap bacteria or microorganisms. Scrapes or cuts in plastic containers can harbor contaminants, too.

There is a variety of sanitizers on the market, and popular choices include the previously mentionedStar-San and Iodophor. Each product has instructions for mixing, soaking, and rinsing, so it is important to read the instructions carefully and follow them for effective sanitation.

Fragrance-free household bleach diluted in water (1 tablespoon bleach per 1 gallon of water) is an effective sanitizer, but many home brewers warn against it. Bleach can react with the phenols in wort and beer to form chlorophenol. This compound gives the beer a medicinal taste and an aroma that is considered a defect. Although bleach can be used, it must be rinsed well and may not be worth the risk of ruining a batch of beer. For details about sanitizing equipment, see page 18, and for more information on each various sanitizing agent, check out the Brewing Introduction on page 48.

Boiling Over

As part of the brewing process, boiling the wort makes the finished product more stable, adds flavor, and kills bacteria. This might seem like a simple step, but you risk boil-over, especially if you're an inexperienced brewer. It's ideal to use a brew kettle with a volume that is one-fourth to one-third greater than the volume of liquid you will boil (not the final volume of liquid for your batch of beer). Pot size can also vary according to whether you're doing a partial or full boil. For example, if you're brewing a 5-gallon batch with a partial boil, a 5-gallon brew kettle will do just fine, but if you'll be doing a full boil with a 5-gallon batch, you'll need a larger kettle—ideally a 6.5-gallon model.

The boiling step requires close attention to prevent boil-over. Controlling the burner at the right time is essential. Just before the wort comes to a full boil, you will see foam accumulate on the surface. Before the wort boils and when the foaming begins, turn down the burner.

Casper recommends skimming some of the foam, referred to as hot break, from the top of the kettle as it accumulates. Once the foam decreases, you can continue to monitor the temperature and boil the wort for the time recommended by your kit or recipe.

Fermentation Problems

During fermentation, yeast converts the sugars in the boiled wort to ethanol, carbon dioxide, and other by-products that contribute to the flavor of the beer. Yeast and temperature control are two important factors for preventing problems during fermentation.

The amount and type of yeast you need varies by recipe. Your local home brew supply store likely can help you choose the best option. Invest in high-quality, fresh yeast and store it in the refrigerator.

Cooling the wort to an ideal fermentation temperature and holding that temperature until fermentation finishes is what Casper considers a very common challenge for home brewers, second only to sanitation issues. This is why it's recommended for beginning home brewers to begin with an ale that ferments at room temperature. Once Casper mastered this, he says that his "consistency [in] repeating the same beer improved tenfold."

Starting out with the right equipment is proactive step in avoiding problems.

Cooling the wort to the appropriate temperature according to your recipe before pitching the yeast is vital to yeast activity. If the wort remains too hot, it can kill the yeast, which prevents fermentation from beginning. Another risk is that the beer will develop one of the dreaded off-flavors (more details later in this chapter). If the wort is too cold when you pitch the yeast, it can go dormant and result in "stuck" fermentation.

A common issue for home brewers of all experience levels is maintaining the beer at the proper temperature for fermentation. Once you've obtained the correct cooling temperature, pitched the yeast, and fermentation has begun, the next step is to control the temperature throughout fermentation. Fermenting beer at too high a temperature can cause unwanted fruity or harsh flavors.

Appropriate fermentation temperatures are determined by the type of beer. Ales are generally fermented at 68 to 72 degrees Fahrenheit, whereas lagers are fermented at 45 to 55 degrees F. The temperature of the room where the beer is fermenting, as well as outdoor temperatures, can influence the fermentation temperature. This is why lagers are often brewed during the winter months and why some home brewers prefer brewing in basements, cellars, or garages, depending on the time of year and the type of beer that they are brewing.

One method for controlling temperature fluctuations involves placing the fermentor in a tub of room-temperature water. If you need to reduce the fermentation temperature, you can add ice to the water bath, but this is a tricky process because you must monitor the temperature closely to ensure that the wort does not get too cold. If you need to raise the fermentation temperature, you can insulate the fermentor by wrapping it in blankets. Electric heating jackets or wraps designed to fit carboys are other options for raising the temperature, but both of these are slightly advanced options. It's best to begin with a style of beer that doesn't require any special treatment in regard to fermentation.

Chill Haze

Chill haze, a haze or cloudiness caused by the presence of various proteins and polyphenols, can form in beer when it is chilled. Although chill haze does not indicate that the beer is spoiled or bad, beer clarity remains an appealing characteristic. It's difficult for home-brewed beers to obtain the same clarity as commercial beers, but you can take a few steps to reduce chill haze.

Ensuring that the wort undergoes a vigorous 60-minute boil helps remove more of the proteins and polyphenols that cause the haze. Cooling the wort quickly after it boils also can remove the haze-causing compounds. Casper recommends investing in a good wort chiller to save time and improve your finished beer.

Adding Irish moss to your boil is another tool for reducing chill haze, Burke says. "I add 1 teaspoon about 15 minutes before the end of my boil, and it clears up the beer," he adds. A species of red algae, Irish moss is available online and at home brew supply stores. It contains carrageenan, which reacts with the proteins during the boil to more effectively remove them from the beer.

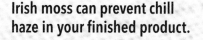

A common issue for home brewers of all experience levels is maintaining the beer at the proper temperature for fermentation.

Contaminants

Beer contamination can occur at any stage of the brewing process, and the signs of contamination are numerous. The beer might develop a tart flavor, a buttery flavor or smell, a medicinal taste or smell, a corn-like flavor, a vinegary aroma, excessive carbonation, or surface mold growth.

Contamination can occur due to the presence of bacteria or exposure to oxygen. Proper sanitation and a correct boil are the two best ways to prevent contaminants. Plastic fermentors often get scratched when cleaning, and these crevices can hold bacteria. Replace scratched fermentors, and consider investing in a glass carboy to reduce contamination.

Irish moss can prevent chill haze in your finished product.

Casper also recommends keeping a tight lid on your fermentor and using an airlock device. Airlock devices prevent oxidation by allowing carbon dioxide to be released without letting air into the fermentor. Also resist the urge to repeatedly open the beer for samples and hydrometer checks. Each time the fermenting beer is exposed to air, you increase the risk for contamination. It's best to just watch the air lock for signs of the end of fermentation, if you can bear it.

Specific Questions

Q: I pitched the yeast, but nothing's happened yet.

A. Have you waited two full days? Yeast takes a little while to start working, and some strains are a bit slower than others, particularly lager strains.

If two days have passed, and you're still not seeing any airlock bubbles, check the seal of your fermentor. If it's not airtight, the carbon dioxide may be escaping through a crack in the lid. If you discover that your fermentor or lid is leaky, it's not a huge deal—your batch should still ferment normally, but you should replace the non-airtight portion of your setup for the next batch.

It's also possible that your yeast is bad. Make sure that you always use fresh yeast whenever possible, and be sure to check the expiration date on your vial of liquid yeast or packets of dry yeast before you pitch it. Additionally, make sure you rehydrate dry yeast before use.

To check if your yeast is active, take another hydrometer reading. If your gravity is lower than it was on bottling day, your yeast is viable; if it's identical, then your yeast isn't working at all.

Finally, make sure that your beer is at the correct fermentation temperature. If your wort is too cold, the yeast will temporarily go dormant and stop working; thankfully, though, readjusting the temperature will wake it back up.

Unfortunately, if you do determine that your yeast is bad, you'll need to start over. The presence of those dead yeast cells will throw off the end flavor of your beer, even if you pitch additional yeast on top.

Q: My beer has a weird flavor. What caused it?

A. Well, first, let's rule out one possible cause that you may have intentionally used: take a look at your yeast strain. Sometimes specific types of yeasts will produce fruity or spicy flavors as a side effect of their use—Belgian yeasts, for example, are often incredibly fruity, producing a banana or clove flavor in beers brewed with them. Check the packaging of your yeast for flavor advice or look it up online to find out if it has any commonly associated flavors with its use. See the yeast section of Chapter 3, Ingredients, for additional information.

If you're still getting an off-flavor that isn't yeast-related, check the chart in this chapter for information on what could have caused the issue and how to correct it, either on this batch or on the next. Some taste issues are fixable with additional fermentation, while others can only be fixed on future batches.

One final note: Some of the flavors listed in the chart are desired in certain beer styles, but if the flavor notes become overpowering, that's when you should take action to halt them in their tracks.

Q: Why is my beer flat?

A: Two major reasons: either you didn't add enough priming sugar before you bottled, or you haven't let your yeast properly work on the priming sugar before you tried your beer. It's best to bottle-condition your beer for two weeks after you bottle to allow the remaining live yeast to work on the new sugar you've added, and if you try the beer before this two-week period is up, the beer can potentially taste sweeter and flatter than the end result will be. Additionally, make sure that you use the recommended amounts of priming sugar to give your beer the proper levels of carbonation.

Properly carbonated beer will have a nice head of foam.

Q: My bottles blew up. How can I avoid this in the future?

A: The first piece of advice I can give you is to be careful when cleaning up after this sort of accident—watch for glass shards, and check corners and edges for puddles of sticky beer. As far as the cause of your explosions, you may have used too much priming sugar before you bottled, or you filled the bottles too full and the carbon dioxide had nowhere to go. Uncap your remaining bottles and reseal them with new, sanitized caps to avoid additional blow-ups from this batch. It's also possible that you bottled before primary fermentation had completed, so make sure that you wait until either you hit your projected final gravity reading, or you don't see any bubbles in the airlock for 48 hours. Finally, it is also possible that you're on the bad end of a wild-yeast infection—taste one of the bottles; if the flavor is off, uncap and dispose of all of your bottles. The last thing you want is additional "bottle grenades" to explode and leave you with a mess of sticky beer and broken glass.

Enjoy the Process

As you become an experienced home brewer, you'll figure out how to prevent the situations that lead to these common problems. Each type of beer is different, however, and every time you brew a new type, you'll experience a learning curve. Don't be surprised if you encounter the same problems from time to time.

"Get the entire process down on a basic level before experimenting too much or jumping to advanced brewing techniques," Casper advises. "This foundation will carry you through all the beers that you brew." He adds that home brewing is supposed to be fun, not stressful, and recommends following an acronym popular among fellow home brewers: RDWHAHB, which stands for "relax, don't worry, and have a home brew."

Troubleshooting Bad Taste

TASTES LIKE	CAUSE	HOW TO FIX IT
Green or rotten apples	Acetaldehyde, an intermediate compound in yeast's formation of alcohol	Any live yeast left in the bottles will likely take care of this— just take the bottles out of the refrigerator, shake them to wake the yeast up, and allow the beer to ferment for a little longer. The acetaldehyde will be further processed and the flavors will disappear.
Medicine	Chlorophenol, a compound built from the presence of chlorine in your batch	This only appears if you use a chlorine-based sanitizer, like bleach, so make sure to rinse extra well before you let any of your equipment touch your wort. You can also rinse with boiled water for an extra precautionary step.
Butter or buttered popcorn	Diacetyl, a natural compound produced by yeast	Diacetyl is typically produced by yeast during the fermentation process and then reabsorbed by yeast cells. Give your beer a few more days before bottling, or, if you've already bottled, shake the bottles lightly and let them sit at room temperature for a few more days before drinking. (These buttery flavors are desirable in some ales, but if they're overpowering, allow the beer to sit.)
Cooked vegetables	Dimethyl sulfide, a compound produced in the malting and heating of grain	This compound is continuously produced in hot wort, and a slowly cooled wort can retain these flavors in the final product. Make sure that you boil your wort for the full hour— these compounds will evaporate out as it boils—and to cool your wort as fast as possible (without risking contamination, of course).
Various types of fruit, especially banana	Esters, a by-product of yeast's fermentation process	You want some fruity flavors in some beer styles, especially Belgian varieties, but if the fruitiness is overpowering, it's possible that you fermented at too high a temperature. Keep your wort fermenting in the correct temperature range for your yeast strain, and be sure to pitch the appropriate amount.
Sulfur	Hydrogen sulfide, a naturally produced chemical during fermentation	All yeast strains produce some hydrogen sulfide as they ferment sugar, but usually the carbon dioxide that is also produced will carry it away into the atmosphere. You may have allowed your beer to sit too long before bottling it, so make sure you're bottling soon after you hit your target final gravity and make sure that you allow carbon dioxide to escape via an airlock during fermentation.

TASTES LIKE	CAUSE	HOW TO FIX IT
Overly sweet/sugary	Maltose, a sugar compound	This is maybe the easiest problem to fix. Your beer just isn't quite done fermenting, so allow the yeast to work a little longer until you hit your projected final gravity. Also, make sure you use high-quality, unspoiled yeast because sometimes spoiled or low-quality yeast will quit early, leaving the maltose in the wort unprocessed.
Skunked beer or burned rubber	Mercaptan, a chemical produced when hops are exposed to ultraviolet light	You know how some of the beers kept in green bottles can occasionally taste skunky? That's because green bottles don't filter out UV light the way that brown glass bottles do. Keep your beer out of direct sunlight at all times and bottle in brown glass bottles for best results.
Mold or mildew	Mold	Keep your fermenting beer stored in a dry place. Moldy flavors in beer are almost always caused by fermentation that takes place in a dank, musty area, like a basement.
Soap	Soap	There are two main causes of soapy flavors in beer: improper rinsing of equipment (which is pretty easy to fix–just rinse better!) and letting beer sit too long in the primary fermentor. The fatty acids in the trub (pronounced troob–the matter left in the fermentor after fermentation ends) begin to break down after they sit too long, so if you're planning to age your beer, make sure you transfer it to a secondary fermentor and only do the primary fermentation for the recommended amount of time.
Vinegar or other strong acidic flavors	Wild yeast	Wild yeast and bacteria are in the air around us at all times, and if your beer has strong acidic flavors, you've likely been hit by an infection. Be sure to keep your fermentor airtight, and up your sanitization regimen, too–you'll get 'em next time.
Yeast	Yeast	If you're getting overpowering yeast flavors, you're likely either tasting the beer too early in the fermenting process or pitching too much yeast. The inverse is also true, however: if "dead" yeast sits too long in beer, it can start to "eat" itself through a process called autolysis. Use the recommended amount of yeast and let it ferment for the recommended amount of time.

Brewers' Stories

Profiles by Wendy Wilson

Every home brewer has a genesis story. Whether an attempt to make a product that couldn't be found on store shelves, a natural evolution of a years-long love of beer, or a simple desire to turn DIY leanings toward alcoholic beverages, the way you begin home brewing is a valuable story to tell, especially if you keep the hobby going for a long time.

The brewers profiled in this chapter have taken their casual hobby and transformed it into commercial operations and competitive awards, but they got their start just like you: simple batches of home-brewed beer in their kitchens. From their hilarious stories of batches gone wrong—shattered carboys and exploded fermentors and flooded kitchens, oh my!—to their sensible advice, these brewers have much to teach, and we have much to learn. And what's better than a primary source for practical advice?

If you need some brewing inspiration after a failed batch or botched recipe, look no further.

Two Shy Brewing

The guys of Two Shy Brewing—Erik Nielsen, Paul Singleton, Jim Little, and Lyle Hruda—started out as award-winning home brewers. But, a couple of years ago, the crew from Roseburg, Oregon, made the jump from hobby to commercial, and they haven't looked back.

"We started home brewing in a friend's garage, and the beer was pretty good," Singleton says. "It was kind of a shock that something we made at home was as good as something that was commercially available, so we kept brewing."

They initially gave their brews to friends and passed them out at local events. Eventually, they developed a following, got some honest feedback, tweaked their recipes, and really started dreaming.

"We kept saying, 'We should open a brewery,'" Nielsen recalls. "One day, we decided to stop dreaming and try to make it a reality."

So they rented a warehouse and got to work. At first, they used their home-brew equipment, but as their fan base grew, they needed to make more beer, so they invested in some commercial tools.

"We just wanted to get going, so [we] did it with what we had," Singleton says. "We had something to sell, something we could be proud of. How we made it, on big stuff or small stuff, wasn't really a concern. It wasn't a concern until we had been doing it a few years and wanted to make a lot more product at a time!"

While making beer and running the brewery, all four of them hold down full-time jobs, but they manage to produce enough suds to keep taps flowing at Two Shy Brewing and in pubs all over town. At any one time, they have six beers available, including Influence IPA, Reformation Red, Phat Odd Stout, Uberdunkelweisen, and Ignition Double IPA.

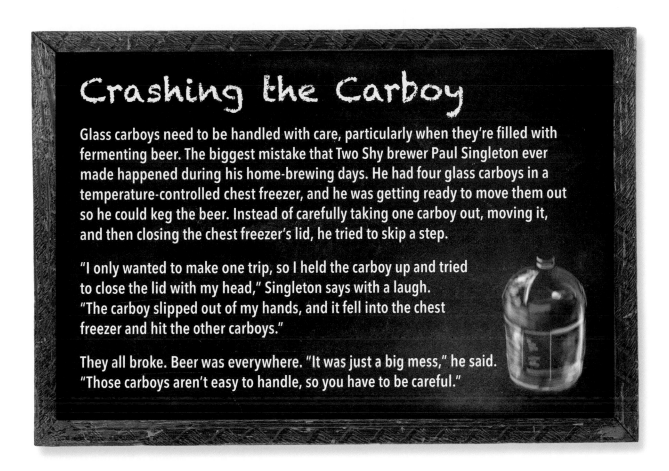

Crashing the Carboy

Glass carboys need to be handled with care, particularly when they're filled with fermenting beer. The biggest mistake that Two Shy brewer Paul Singleton ever made happened during his home-brewing days. He had four glass carboys in a temperature-controlled chest freezer, and he was getting ready to move them out so he could keg the beer. Instead of carefully taking one carboy out, moving it, and then closing the chest freezer's lid, he tried to skip a step.

"I only wanted to make one trip, so I held the carboy up and tried to close the lid with my head," Singleton says with a laugh. "The carboy slipped out of my hands, and it fell into the chest freezer and hit the other carboys."

They all broke. Beer was everywhere. "It was just a big mess," he said. "Those carboys aren't easy to handle, so you have to be careful."

"Ignition has been our most sought-after [brew]," Singleton says. "It's been surprisingly accepted even among people who don't like IPAs. There's something about it."

The Two Shy crew hopes eventually to move from kegs to bottles. "It's a necessary step in getting our stuff out," Singleton says. "Bottles are convenient. It's easy to take a six-pack with you."

For now, though, they welcome Roseburg-area beer lovers in their tasting room and happily fill their pint glasses and empty growlers.

James McNulty

James McNulty of Whitsett, North Carolina, started home brewing with his father in 2010. With that solid foundation, he set out on his own—and took bronze at the American Homebrewers Association's 2014 National Homebrew Competition for his Brett Beer.

"One of the best things about home brewing is that you can constantly evolve," says McNulty, whose first home-brew attempt was a William's Brewing California Common extract kit.

He says two of the biggest changes to his technique were moving from extract to all-grain brewing and converting an old dorm refrigerator into a fermentation chamber.

"The all-grain brewing allowed me to have a lot more control over my recipes and the final product," he says, "and the refrigerator allowed me to control my fermentation temperatures. This made my beer so much more consistent and has allowed me to brew almost any style."

McNulty's style of choice: Munich Helles. "I like to brew a lot of German-style lagers, but I also really like to brew saisons," he adds. "They're a great style [to] experiment with."

As a home-brew hobbyist, McNulty has learned several valuable lessons. "Keep really good records during the entire brewing, packaging, and tasting process," he recommends. "It's really hard to brew consistently if you aren't good at keeping records. This will also help you figure out why a beer might have not turned out quite right, or it can help you recreate a great recipe time after time."

He also learned to take care of his workers. "Your yeasts are the ones that ultimately make the beer," he says. "You want to create an optimal environment for them to do their work, whether it is making a starter to ensure a proper cell count, mashing at the right temperature to get the right mix of long- and short-chain sugars, or controlling your fermentation temperature so that there is as little stress on the yeast as possible. The best recipe in the world is worthless if your yeasts are not happy."

The most important wisdom McNulty shares: Have fun while you brew. "Brew days should be fun and stress-free," he says. "Very few mistakes will ruin your beer. It might not be the best batch, but it will still most likely be pretty good."

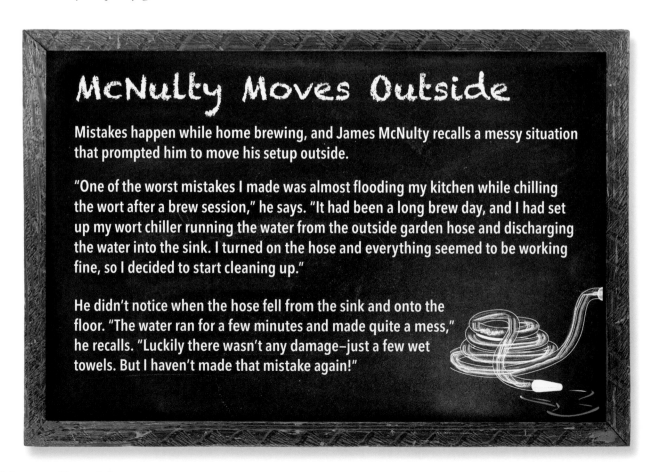

McNulty Moves Outside

Mistakes happen while home brewing, and James McNulty recalls a messy situation that prompted him to move his setup outside.

"One of the worst mistakes I made was almost flooding my kitchen while chilling the wort after a brew session," he says. "It had been a long brew day, and I had set up my wort chiller running the water from the outside garden hose and discharging the water into the sink. I turned on the hose and everything seemed to be working fine, so I decided to start cleaning up."

He didn't notice when the hose fell from the sink and onto the floor. "The water ran for a few minutes and made quite a mess," he recalls. "Luckily there wasn't any damage—just a few wet towels. But I haven't made that mistake again!"

Frank Barickman

In 1999, Frank Barickman received a home-brewing kit for his birthday. Fifteen years later, he has amassed 250 awards for his beers, including a second-place win in the final round of the 2014 American Homebrewers Association's National Homebrew Competition with his Dark American Lager.

His secret is practice—and lots of it.

"It's like any hobby or sport," says Barickman, who lives in Delaware, Ohio. "The more you do it, the more you learn, and hopefully the better you become. Though I have done a bunch of reading, I found that my brewing expertise greatly evolved just by brewing frequently. This allowed me to better understand what the different types of grains, hops, and yeasts contributed to the final product. It's one thing to read about it; it's a better thing to try it."

From India pale ales and cream ales to dark English milds and foreign extra stouts and everything in between, Barickman has brewed all sorts of beers. He has also worked with commercial breweries in central Ohio to develop recipes, solve technical problems, and collaborate on beers for the Great American Beer Festival.

Before brewing a particular beer, Barickman learns about its style and researches the grains, hops, water chemistry, yeast, and fermentation schedule he plans to use.

"Styles are sometimes created by changing ingredients, but others are created by the process," he says. "Sometimes my efforts miss the mark, but then I reevaluate the ingredients and process I used and make changes to help improve the beer I was attempting to make. I am still searching for the perfect IPA!"

As Barickman has grown in his hobby, he has upgraded his equipment numerous times and continuously "tweaks his system," he says.

"I now brew on a 15-gallon system that consists of some professional 20-gallon vessels," he notes. "I have a brewing stand that I custom-built with propane burners and various accessories, like pumps, a chiller, and thermometers. I've upgraded most of my plastic buckets that were used as fermentors to

Barickman's Biggest Blunder

Although Frank Barickman is an award-winning home brewer, he still has made his share of mistakes, including brewing an explosive batch of beer that taught him the value of a blow-off tube. He was brewing a Russian imperial stout, a large-gravity beer with lots of fermentable sugar in the wort, and he overpitched his yeast.

"I pitched about ten times—yes, ten times—what I would normally pitch in a regular beer," he says. "I was using buckets to ferment this beer, and they have a tight seal with a gasket so that air cannot get into the fermenting wort. There is a small hole where you attach an airlock that allows the CO_2 to escape but prevents air from coming in as the beer ferments."

While the beer was fermenting, Barickman found himself too busy to check its progress. He didn't realize that the airlock had clogged with yeast.

"About two days into it, I heard a large 'bang' at 3 a.m.," he said. "My fermentors had both exploded, and 10 gallons of beer were coating the room from floor to ceiling. Beer went everywhere. Not only did I lose the batch, but I had many hours of cleaning up."

He now uses a blow-off tube for big fermentations. "A blow-off tube allows for a larger diameter hole so that it will not clog," Barickman says, "and this prevents building pressure in the vessel. Thank goodness it was a plastic bucket versus a glass carboy!"

glass carboys, and now I even have a few stainless-steel conicals that are similar to what commercial breweries use. Many home brewers geek out about their equipment and find it just as much fun to plan their next upgrade."

Barickman has three tips for home brewers: control your temperature while fermenting, don't over-dry-hop, and pitch large amounts of healthy yeast.

"And if you want to improve your beer and win more awards, learn to judge," says Barickman, a Beer Judge Certification Program Grand Master II judge. "Blind tasting, understanding the aromas and flavors you are perceiving, and knowing what causes them will greatly improve your beer. Having to judge different categories teaches you about the styles. You learn what works and what does not work."

Josanna Dixon

Josanna Dixon of Burlington, Kentucky, admits that she started brewing beer to meet men. "I had some friends who started home brewing as a hobby, and I tagged along to see what it was all about," she recalls. "I would never date anyone who did not drink. There's nothing like enjoying good company with great conversation over an exceptional beer. I'm happy to report that it worked; I met my husband at a brew-out."

Brewing since 1996, Dixon loves to cook up English special bitter and German wheat beer, adding fruits like apricot or cherry to the mix. "I knew this was no ordinary hobby from my first batch," says Dixon, who also makes cider. "I enjoy cooking and tweaking recipes, and beer took that obsession to another level. Why not use the same creativity in beer and cider?"

As with most home brewers, Dixon's first beer was from a kit. "I requested it as a Christmas present," she says. "I sent my mother to the [now-closed] Winemaker Shop in Fort Worth with a shopping list. She got me everything I needed for a southern brown. It wasn't fantastic, but it was a great start."

Sanitation is key to home brewing, Dixon notes. "Without good techniques, your best beer will not turn out as you wanted."

Her advice to hobby brewers: take your time and enjoy the experience. "Do not rush it," she says. "You can take an entire day and leave your other life behind. When you're home brewing, don't worry about anything but what you're doing right now."

Dixon also encourages brewers to connect with a local home-brew club. "With the sharing of ideas and processes, you learn from the trial and error of others," she says. "You have a chance to get together and enjoy a common love of brewing.

"You will have members old and young, experienced and newbies," she says. "What do you have to lose? You also get the bonus of making some great friends along the way. I couldn't imagine not having my brewing friends in my life."

Award-Winning Disaster

Josanna Dixon's worst home-brewing foible happened during her first solo batch. "I scalded my foot with the hot water return from my immersion wort chiller," she recalls, "and I spent the rest of the brew day with my foot in a bucket of ice water, finishing the beer."

Despite working with an injury, the beer turned out to be award-winning. "The final results won me my very first medal at the 1999 CMI Oktobersbest [Home Brew] Competition, a first place in the Belgian strong ale category," Dixon says.

13

Next Steps

So you've made and enjoyed your first batch of home-brewed beer. Your friends have patted you on the back; you've basked in the glory of turning barley, hops, and water into one of mankind's most favorite beverages; and now you're hooked on the hobby, right? So, now what?

I'm glad you asked. The fun and excitement of home brewing doesn't have to end when the final bottle of your batch is finished. In fact, that first batch should just be the tip of the iceberg because home brewing's rabbit hole goes much, much deeper. The following suggestions are some ways to take your hobby to the next level. Feel free to approach these incrementally or just jump right in and go whole-hog—remember, half the fun of home brewing is experimentation, particularly once you have the basics under your belt.

Repeat Batches

The first thing I encourage you to do is repeat the entire process so that you can get a better handle on it. Before you start trying some crazy innovations or wild ingredient additions, you need to have mastered the basics. Try brewing a few of the basic beer styles, like one of the colored ales (pale, brown, or amber) or a porter, to broaden your range. Also, stick with ales at first, because lagers need to be fermented at such low temperatures that they require additional equipment. Plus, there isn't much sense in trying to brew a fancy double dry-hopped India pale ale (IPA) when you've never brewed an IPA in the first place.

Making one or two more basic batches is a great way to get a solid foundation of extract brewing under your belt. Sticking with a starter kit for your first few batches is recommended, too. Then, one of the first steps you can take into deeper water is to brew without an ingredient kit.

If it takes only one additional batch to get yourself to the point where you feel comfortable with the brewing process, that's excellent, but just don't get overconfident and take on more than you can handle. Not only is a spoiled batch of beer a waste of time, but it's also a waste of money, particularly if you're using expensive additional ingredients, such as honey, or making a beer style that's heavy on the inputs, such as a barleywine or imperial IPA.

Rethink Equipment

Once you're a few batches in, you should start thinking about how your operation can be streamlined. Are there optional pieces of equipment that you've been considering, like a wort chiller, portable stove, or kegerator? If you plan to keep developing your home-brewing skills and pursuing this hobby, go for it. By now, you should have a pretty good idea of what would help you make beer faster or more efficiently, so add those pieces of equipment in as you see fit. If you're on the fence about a piece of equipment, don't make an investment in it without a little research. There are a plethora of home-brewing forums online, and the staffers at your local home-brewing supply store are an excellent resource, too.

Get to a point where you're comfortable with your setup and what it allows you to do. It's not a great idea to try too many new steps, ingredients, or pieces of equipment in one single batch. Instead of going all-grain on your first force-carbonated dunkel, consider trying just one of those three novel pieces to keep yourself on track and avoid any mishaps.

Develop Recipes

Once you've got the process and your equipment setup down to the point where you're comfortable, cut the apron strings completely, so to speak, and start developing your own recipes. Have you ever had crazy ideas about blending beer styles or adding fruits, vegetables, or nuts to a batch? Go for it! There's nothing holding you back but your imagination. I recommend doing some quick research before jumping in willy-nilly, however. If you've got a craving for a papaya IPA, for example, somebody else might have done one before and may have some tips on when to add the papaya or how much to include. (Check out Chapter 3, Ingredients, for some additional ingredient ideas to add to your home brews.)

Recipe creation is much more than just throwing in some extra flavors, though—you can play around with yeast strains and grain bills to craft your perfect brews. If you like your pale ales to be a touch darker than most, trying using a darker extract variety. For heavier carbonation, try a more active yeast. When you home brew, you're able to try some of those flavor combinations that you've never seen in stores, and the stakes are pretty low in the grand scheme of things. It's also an excellent

idea to try smaller batches for some of your more outlandish creations (check out Chapter 9, Small-Batch Brewing, for more information on scaling down your batches). Think of smaller batches as trial runs for your more experimental recipes.

Go All-Grain

A major step that offers you more control of the flavor and colors of your beers is ditching the extract and going all-grain. This method provides you with the most flexibility and control over creating an individual wort, and mastering the all-grain method will equip you with the skills you need to recreate any beer you can find commercially. (Well, maybe not the ones brewed with wild yeast, but those are best left to the professionals anyway.)

Broaden Your Scale

In the inverse of small-batch brewing, you can choose to upscale your batches and make more beer with every brewing cycle. (Check out one of the recipe calculators listed in the Resources for more information on scaling up a recipe for a larger batch.)

If upscaling each individual batch doesn't appeal to you, consider investing in another fermentor or two and have multiple batches going in rotation. This lends itself very well to small-batch brewing; you might find yourself quickly overwhelmed by beer if you have multiple 5-gallon batches going at once!

Go Commercial

This is the dream, right? If you really like brewing beer, and you have the financial means and time to devote to running your own business, start thinking about expanding into the commercial market. But, before you do, be sure to do your research—rules and regulations governing alcohol sales are notoriously strict, and you have to truly know what you're doing to keep a massive batch of beer properly sanitized and tasty. Check out the interview with the guys behind Two Shy Brewing in Chapter 12, Brewers' Stories, for more information on making the leap.

No matter how you choose to keep developing your hobby, the major factors in your next-step decisions should be your level of comfort and your level of enjoyment. If all-grain seems too intimidating to you, don't bother with it! Extract beers are still delicious, and you can always work your way up to all-grain batches later. Similarly, if you don't feel creative enough yet to develop your own recipes, don't—you're no more or less a home brewer if you use recipes to brew your beer instead of crafting your own, no matter what the trolls on home-brewing forums say. The worlds of craft beer and home brewing are inclusive, not exclusive, so kudos to you for brewing beer in the first place. The more you enjoy the process, the more likely you'll be to keep brewing beer.

14

Beer Recipes

Now that you've got a solid handle on the home-brewing process, let's get into the nitty-gritty of specific beers. This chapter is chock-full of recipes for ales and lagers, and even instructions for a California Common, a hybrid style brewed with lager yeast at ale temperatures.

The recipes are organized by two major categories: type of beer (ale or lager) and type of recipe (extract or all-grain). (There are also two gluten-free recipes and the aforementioned hybrid beer as well.) Remember that all-grain recipes require additional steps and are slightly more difficult than extract recipes, so it's best to begin on the extract level. For most of the all-grain recipes, however, you'll also find extract instructions in the recipes, so all of these recipes are within a beginning or intermediate home brewer's grasp.

You'll note that a lot of the instructions in the recipes are pretty vague because they assume that you understand the home-brewing process. So, when you see instructions like "Carbonate and bottle," feel free to accomplish these steps however you'd like. For beginning home brewers, the methods discussed in the earlier chapters are your best bet (bottle-conditioning instead of force-carbonating, etc.). If you run across an unfamiliar term, check out the glossary at the back of this book.

One important thing to keep in mind: recipes are guidelines for making beer. If your predicted final gravity is lower than the recipe says it should be, your beer is far from ruined—this just means that your alcohol level is going to be slightly higher than projected. Similarly, if your original gravity is lower than projected, your beer will be slightly less alcoholic.

You can use these recipes verbatim or as stepping stones to customized batches—just remember that these recipes have been tested and verified, so if you want to make a batch that you know will turn out right, give one of these a try before swapping out hop varieties or throwing in additional flavoring ingredients.

Once you're comfortable with following a recipe, start experimenting with recipe creation.

Terms and Definitions

Alcohol by volume (ABV):
What percentage of your beer's total volume is alcohol. Most styles of beer will land between 3 and 8 percent.

Alpha acid (AA):
Resin in hops that affects the bitterness of the beer (higher AA content = more bitter).

Batch size:
The size of your final volume of beer. Remember that you'll get roughly ten 12-ounce bottles of beer per gallon.

Final gravity (FG):
A measurement of how much sugar remains after fermentation. The greater the distance between your OG and your FG, the more alcoholic your beer will be.

International bitterness units (IBUs):
Ranging from 0 to 120, this is a measurement of how bitter your beer will be. The lower the number, the less bitter the beer.

Original gravity (OG):
A measurement of the amount of sugar in the wort before fermentation.

Ales

The Alpha Fish Imperial India Pale Ale

By Scott Mansfield

Batch size: 6 gallons
Original gravity: 1.083
Final gravity: 1.031
International bitterness units: 132
Alcohol by volume: 6.8 percent

Forget turning it up to 11. This award-winning Imperial IPA turns the bittering volume up to 13. A big, West Coast-style double IPA, the Alpha Fish was brewed collaboratively by Central Oregon Homebrewers Organization, taking second place in the 2009 Hop Madness: Best Damn Hoppy Beer Competition.

The recipe was submitted by Sunriver Brewing Co. brewmaster Brett Thomas, who describes it as "radically hoppy with big notes of pine resin, fresh-cut tangerines and peaches, and tropical white wine." It's a bit more challenging to brew than a simple malt extract, but Thomas says it's worth the extra effort. "This is certainly one of the most unique double IPAs that I've ever brewed," he adds.

Ingredients

2 gallons water

Milled grains:
½ lb. Crystal 15L malt
¼ lb. Crystal 40L malt

Extracts:
12 lbs. Pilsner malt extract
1¼ lbs. dextrose

Pre-boil hops:
¼ oz. New Zealand Nelson Sauvin pellets
¾ oz. Amarillo pellets
¼ oz. New Zealand Green Bullet pellets

Bittering hops:
1¼ oz. Summit pellets: boil for 60 minutes

Aroma hops:
2 oz. Amarillo pellets: boil for 10 minutes
2 oz. Amarillo pellets: add at flame out

Yeast:
2 packets Safale US-05 dry yeast

Dry hops:
½ oz. Summit pellets
2 oz. Amarillo pellets
½ oz. New Zealand Green Bullet pellets
1 oz. New Zealand Nelson Sauvin pellets

Procedure

1. Steep the milled grains in a grain bag in 2 gallons of 160 degree F water for 30 minutes.

2. Remove the grains and turn up the heat.

3. When the water reaches 180 degrees F, stir in the malt extracts and then add the pre-boil hops.

4. After 30 minutes of boiling, add the bittering hops.

5. After 80 cumulative minutes of boiling, add the first round of aroma hops.

6. After 90 total minutes of boiling, turn off the heat and add the second round of aroma hops.

7. Steep for 5 minutes and then pour the wort through a strainer into the primary fermentor.

8. Add water to equal 6 gallons.

9. Aerate (stir) and chill/cool and then pitch the yeast.

10. Ferment for 14 days.

11. Rack to a secondary fermentor and add the dry hops.

12. When fermentation is complete (about one week later), carbonate and bottle.

Alvord Hefeweizen

By Scott Mansfield

Batch size: 5 gallons
Original gravity: 1.055
Final gravity: 1.044
International bitterness units: 13
Alcohol by volume: 5.4 percent

This all-extract, extra-easy American-style wheat beer recipe was developed by a longtime Oregon-based home brewer for a camping trip to the Alvord Desert outside of Fields, Oregon—population thirteen. He describes it as "clean, light, and refreshing with added lemon." In other words, it's the perfect refreshment for cutting through playa dust.

Ingredients

2 gallons water

Extracts:
  7 lbs. liquid malt extract: 55 percent barley, 45 percent wheat

Adjuncts:
  1½ tsp. gypsum
  ½ tsp. sea salt

Bittering hops:
  1 oz. Hallertauer hops: boil for 60 minutes

Aroma hops:
  1 oz. Hallertauer hops: steep for 5 minutes

Yeast:
  1 "smack pack" Wyeast Brewer's Choice American Wheat yeast

Priming sugar:
  ¾ cup corn sugar

Procedure

1. Add the liquid malt extract to 2 gallons of almost boiling water and stir.

2. When the water boils, add the gypsum, sea salt, and bittering hops.

3. After 60 minutes, turn off the heat.

4. Add the aroma hops and steep for 5 minutes.

5. Pour the wort through a strainer into the primary fermentor.

6. Add water to equal 5 gallons.

7. Aerate (stir) and chill/cool and then pitch the yeast.

8. Ferment for 1 to 2 weeks or until activity stops.

9. Rack to the secondary fermentor and condition for 1 to 2 weeks.

10. Add the corn sugar, carbonate, and bottle.

American IPA

By Scott Mansfield

Batch size: 5 gallons
Original gravity: 1.065
Final gravity: 1.020
International bitterness units: 90
Alcohol by volume: 6.0 percent

This easy-to-drink American-style IPA recipe was submitted by Jon Abernathy, an Oregon-based home brewer and beer blogger at The Brew Site (www.thebrewsite.com). He says that it brings the aroma of the classic American hop, Cascade, to the forefront, "particularly if you dry-hop it." He encourages home brewers to play with the bittering hops in this recipe, saying that "any high-alpha-acid variety will play well here. If you can find it, try Sorachi Ace for a lemony character, or use Warrior or Horizon hops for additional intriguing profiles."

Ingredients

2 gallons water

Milled grains:
½ lb. 10L Crystal malt
½ lb. 40L Crystal malt
¼ lb. Biscuit malt

Extracts:
7 lbs. light malt extract syrup
1¼ lbs. light dry malt extract

Bittering hops:
¾ oz. Centennial hops: boil for 60 minutes
¾ oz. Nugget or other high-alpha American hops: boil for 60 minutes
¼ oz. Centennial hops: boil for 45 minutes
¼ oz. Nugget hops: boil for 45 minutes

Aroma hops:
1 oz. Cascade hops: boil for 15 minutes
1 oz. Cascade hops: boil for 15 minutes

Dry hops:
1 oz. Cascade hops (optional)

Yeast:
1 packet Wyeast Northwest Ale yeast strain 1332

Priming sugar:
¾ cup corn sugar for priming

Procedure

1. Steep the grains in a nylon mesh bag in 2 gallons of water as it heats to a boil.

2. When the water reaches about 180 degrees F, take out the grain bag and remove the pot from the heat.

3. Add the extracts, stirring to dissolve thoroughly.

4. Return to the heat and bring to a boil.

5. Once the mixture boils, add the first portion of Centennial and Nugget hops.

6. After 15 minutes, add the second round of Centennial and Nugget hops.

7. After 45 minutes of boiling, add the first portion of Cascade hops (the aroma hops).

8. After 55 minutes of boiling, add the second portion of Cascade hops.

9. Boil for 5 minutes and then turn off the heat.

10. Pour the wort through a strainer into the primary fermentor.

11. Add water to equal 5 gallons.

12. Aerate (stir) and chill/cool and then pitch the yeast.

13. Ferment for 5 to 7 days as needed.

14. Rack to the secondary fermentor and add the dry hops (if using).

15. Condition for 1 to 2 weeks before bottling, using the corn sugar for priming.

16. Bottle-condition for at least 2 weeks.

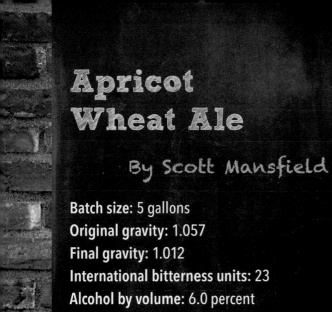

Apricot Wheat Ale

By Scott Mansfield

Batch size: 5 gallons
Original gravity: 1.057
Final gravity: 1.012
International bitterness units: 23
Alcohol by volume: 6.0 percent

Brewing with fruit can be a challenge for beginning brewers. There are several schools of thought on how to use the fruit, how much of it to use, and when to add it to the brew. For this recipe, home brewer and beer blogger John Abernathy (www.TheBrewSite.com) says, "I prefer adding the fruit to the secondary fermentor to preserve as much of the fruit flavor as possible because during primary fermentation, the release of carbon dioxide tends to scrub out the flavors." Wheat ales provide a palatable base for just about any aromatic fruit, so have fun experimenting with cherries, strawberries, or raspberries.

Ingredients

5 gallons water

Milled grains:
½ lb. Crystal malt

Extracts:
7 lbs. wheat malt extract syrup
1 lb. rice syrup solids

Bittering hops:
1 oz. Cascade hops: boil for 60 minutes

Adjuncts:
5-10 lbs. frozen apricots, halved and pitted

Yeast:
Wyeast American Ale yeast
strain 1056

Priming sugar:
¾ cup corn sugar

Procedure

1. Steep the grains in a nylon mesh bag placed in the water and bring to a boil.

2. When the temperature reaches about 180 degrees F, remove the grain bag.

3. Remove the brewing pot from the heat and add the wheat extract and rice syrup solids, stirring to dissolve thoroughly.

4. Return to the heat, bring to a boil, and add the bittering hops.

5. Boil for 60 minutes and then turn off the heat and remove.

6. Pour the wort through a strainer into the primary fermentor.

7. Add water to equal 5 gallons.

8. Aerate (stir) and chill/cool and then pitch the yeast.

9. Ferment for 5 to 7 days or until fermentation stops.

10. Rack to a secondary fermentor and add the fruit.

11. After 7 days (or longer if the fruit continues to cause fermentation), either rack off/transfer the fruit to a tertiary fermentor to clarify or bottle.

12. Carbonate with priming sugar and bottle-condition at least 2 weeks before drinking.

Black IPA

By Scott Mansfield

Batch size: 6 gallons
Original gravity: 1.074
Final gravity: 1.020
International bitterness units: 80
Alcohol by volume: 7.0 percent

Black IPA was an emerging style when Brett Thomas created this home-brew recipe. He designed it to emulate Turmoil, brewed by Barley Brown's Beer, and then scaled it up for several test batches at Silver Moon Brewing in Bend, Oregon, where he was head brewer. Eventually, it became their Asmodeus Black IPA. Thomas describes it as "very dark in color, with a medium mouthfeel and an exceptionally fruity, hoppy finish."

Ingredients

2 gallons water

Milled grains:
1 lb. Weyermann Carafa II malt
½ lb. Crystal 40L malt
½ lb. Munich malt

Extracts:
10 lbs. Pilsner malt extract
1 lb. dextrose

Pre-boil hops:
¼ oz. Cascade pellets
¼ oz. Amarillo pellets

Bittering hops:
¾ oz. Summit pellets: boil for 60 minutes
½ oz. Centennial pellets: boil for 30 minutes

Aroma hops:
1 oz. Cascade pellets: boil for 5 minutes
1 oz. Amarillo pellets: boil for 5 minutes
1 oz. Cascade pellets: add at flame out.
1 oz. Amarillo pellets: add at flame out.

Yeast:
2 packets Safale US-05 dried yeast

Dry hops:
1½ oz. Simcoe pellets
1½ oz. Columbus pellets

Procedure

1. Steep the milled grains in a muslin bag in 2 gallons of 160-degree F water for 30 minutes.

2. Remove the grains and turn up the heat.

3. When the water reaches 180 degrees F, stir in the malt extracts and then add the pre-boil hops.

4. After 30 minutes of boiling, add the Summit hops.

5. After 60 total minutes of boiling, add the Centennial hops.

6. After 85 cumulative minutes of boiling, add the first round of aroma hops (Cascade and Amarillo).

7. After 90 total minutes of boiling, turn off the heat and add the second round of aroma hops (Cascade and Amarillo).

8. Pour the wort through a strainer into a primary fermentor.

9. Add water to equal 6 gallons.

10. Aerate (stir) and chill/cool and then pitch the yeast.

11. Ferment at 68 degrees F for 14 days.

12. Rack to a secondary fermentor on day 14 and add the dry hops.

13. Chill to 34 degrees F on day 21.

14. Carbonate and bottle.

Chronic Stout

By Scott Mansfield

Batch size: 5 gallons
Original gravity: 1.076
Final gravity: 1.019
International bitterness units: 54
Alcohol by volume: 7.2 percent

Developed by a North Carolina home brewer, this smooth and creamy stout is the kind of beer that exceeds taste expectations at bottling and improves as it ages. It is delightful after 6 months, delicious at 12 months, and deeply addictive at 18 months. The flavor peaks at about two years of age, assuming you've stored it in a dark, cool environment.

Ingredients

2 gallons water

Milled grains:
1 lb. roasted malt
½ lb. chocolate malt

Extracts:
7 lbs. amber malt extract syrup
2 lbs. dark dried malt extract

Bittering hops:
1 oz. Chinook pellets: boil for 60 minutes

Adjuncts:
1½ tsp. gypsum
½ tsp. sea salt

Aroma hops:
1 oz. Cascade pellets: boil for 10 minutes

Yeast:
1 packet Wyeast Irish Ale yeast strain 1084

Extras:
½ lb. organic Guatemalan cold-brewed coffee (see below*)

Procedure

1. Steep the grains for 30 minutes in 2 gallons of 160- to 170- degree F water.

2. Remove the grains, heat the water, and stir in the extracts just before boiling.

3. Once the mixture boils, add the bittering hops, gypsum, and sea salt.

4. After 40 minutes of boiling, add the aroma hops.

5. After 60 total minutes of boiling, turn off the heat.

6. Pour the wort through a strainer into the primary fermentor.

7. Add water to equal 4½ gallons.

8. Aerate (stir) and chill the wort. Add the coffee and pitch the yeast (add it to the wort).

9. Rack to a carboy after about 1 week; bottle when fermentation stops.

10. Resist the urge to pop open a bottle for at least six months.

*The night before brewing, place the coffee in a half-gallon container with cold water and stir. Chill overnight in the refrigerator and filter before adding to the beer.

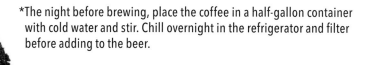

History shows that Bavarian brewers were the first to brew a style of beer that became *weissbier*, or "white beer," named for the light color that wheat gives to beer. Over time, this style has morphed into *hefeweizen*, or "yeast wheat." There are other branches in this particular part of the beer family tree, including styles such as *grätzer* (a smoked wheat beer of Polish descent), *krystalweiss* (named for the clarity of the end product), and Gose or Berliner weisse (a soured wheat beer).

Flavorwise, it's not uncommon for phenols from the yeast to be prominent, especially if the resulting beer is of the Germanic style as opposed to the American style. Hop flavor and aroma are nonexistent. Commercial examples include La Cumbre Brewing Company's A Slice of Hefen, Harpoon Brewery's UFO Hefeweizen, and Sierra Nevada Brewing Company's Kellerweis Hefeweizen.

If you can brew an all-grain version of a hefeweizen, do so; the end product will be lighter in color when compared to an extract-with-grains version. Historically, weizens called for an advanced mashing technique called *decoction mashing*, in which a fraction of the mash is pulled out at set intervals and boiled for a short period of time before being returned to the mash vessel. However, with the grains that a home brewer can get today, decoction mashing is not needed because extraction capability is much higher than what was available a few centuries ago.

"Smack Packs"

A word on the Wyeast packages of yeast: The yeast in these packages is in a smaller plastic bag, which is immersed in a small amount of wort. Activation starts by breaking the yeast package inside, hence the nickname "smack pack."

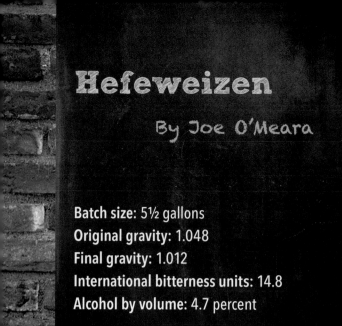

Hefeweizen

By Joe O'Meara

Batch size: 5½ gallons
Original gravity: 1.048
Final gravity: 1.012
International bitterness units: 14.8
Alcohol by volume: 4.7 percent

Ingredients

Yeast:
1 smack pack Wyeast Weihenstephan Weizen yeast strain 3068

3 gallons water

1 lb. flaked wheat

5 lbs. wheat dried malt extract

Bittering hops:
1 oz. Hallertau hops (5 percent AA): boil for 60 minutes

⅔ **cup corn sugar (for bottling)**

Procedure

1. Two days prior to brewing, break the Wyeast smack pack.

2. Heat the water to 155 degrees Fahrenheit. Remove from the heat and add the flaked wheat to a nylon grain bag; steep for 30 to 45 minutes. Remove the grain bag and drain it into the pot.

3. Bring the wort to a boil and then remove it from the heat temporarily.

4. In a separate pot, add the wheat dried malt extract. Then slowly add 1 to 1½ gallons of the wort to the dried malt extract, stirring constantly until dissolved. Add this to the boil vessel.

5. Bring back to a boil. Total boil time is 60 minutes.

6. Add the bittering hops.

7. After 60 minutes, cool to 70 degrees F, add enough water to get to 5½ gallons wort, and pitch the yeast.

8. Ferment for five days and then transfer (rack) to your secondary fermentation vessel. After an additional 7 days, bottle and age for 1 to 2 weeks before enjoying.

Mosaic Double IPA

By Scott Mansfield

Batch size: 5 gallons
Original gravity: 1.076
Final gravity: 1.028
International bitterness units: 71
Alcohol by volume: 7.4 percent

The following double IPA recipe is fairly straightforward, allowing the juicy, tropical Mosaic hops to play a starring role. The familiar piney aroma gives it away as a Simcoe offspring, but the mango, lemon, citrus, and stone-fruit flavors set this varietal apart from its parentage. Packing this or any other single hop into an IPA helps you better understand and appreciate the qualities it can contribute.

Ingredients

2 gallons water

Milled grains:
  6 lbs. pale malt, Maris Otter

Extract:
  6 lbs. pale liquid malt extract

Adjuncts:
  1 tsp. gypsum

Bittering hops:
  1½ oz. Mosaic hop pellets: boil for 60 minutes
  1 oz. Mosaic hop pellets: boil for 30 minutes

Aroma hops:
  1 oz. Mosaic hop pellets: boil for 5 minutes
  1 oz. Mosaic hop pellets: steep for 5 minutes

Yeast:
  1 pack Wyeast American Ale II yeast strain 1272

Priming sugar:
  ¾ cup corn sugar

Procedure

1. Steep the grains in a muslin bag in 2 gallons of 160- to 170-degree F water for 30 minutes.

2. Remove the grains, heat the water to 180 degrees F, stir in the malt extract, and bring to a boil.

3. When the mixture boils, add gypsum and the initial bittering hops.

4. After 30 minutes, add the second round of bittering hops.

5. After 55 total minutes, add the initial aroma hops.

6. After 60 cumulative minutes, turn off the heat and add the final aroma hops.

7. Steep for 5 minutes and then pour the wort through a strainer into the primary fermentor.

8. Add water to 5 gallons.

9. Aerate (stir) and chill the wort and then pitch the yeast.

10. Ferment at 68 degrees F for 10 days or until fermentation stops.

11. Rack to a secondary fermentor and condition for 1 to 2 weeks before adding the corn sugar.

12. Bottle-condition for 2 weeks.

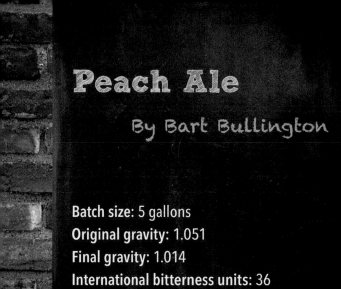

Peach Ale

By Bart Bullington

Batch size: 5 gallons
Original gravity: 1.051
Final gravity: 1.014
International bitterness units: 36
Alcohol by volume: 5.2 percent

I'm personally not a big fan of most fruit beers out there, so I went about creating one that finishes on the hops like an ale should. The slight peach accentuates the beer flavor instead of covering it up. It is dry with a snap of peach and a crisp hop finish.

Ingredients

7½ gallons water

Milled grains:
  1 lb. Crystal malt 40L
  1 lb. Carafoam malt

Extract:
  6 lbs. two-row or liquid malt extract

Adjuncts:
  2 lbs. peach purée

Bittering hops:
  1 oz. Northern Brewer hops

Finishing and aroma hops:
  3 oz. Cascade hop, divided

Yeast:
  2 oz. Windsor or Mauribrew yeast

Procedure:

1. Steep the grains in 160- to 164- degree F water for 30 to 40 minutes. Add the malt extract at the onset of the boil. If all-grain brewing, steep for 60 minutes.

2. Bring to a boil.

3. For partial grain, add the liquid malt extract when the water comes to a boil.

4. As the liquid boils, set a timer for 60 minutes. Add the peach purée and bittering hops.

5. When 20 minutes remain, add 1 oz. Cascade hops.

6. When no time remains, add 2 oz. Cascade hops.

7. Remove from the heat and stir to aerate for 10 to 20 minutes.

8. Cool to 70 to 80 degrees F.

9. Transfer into the fermentation vessel.

10. Add the yeast.

11. Ferment for 10 to 14 days at 64 to 70 degrees F.

12. Cold-condition for 3 to 4 days at 34 to 36 degrees F.

Porter

By Joe O'Meara

Batch size: 5 gallons
Original gravity: 1.055
Final gravity: 1.104
International bitterness units: 34
Alcohol by volume: 5.3 percent

Porter is a beer style rich in history as well as flavor. First mentioned in the 1720s, this style is very similar to stout in terms of appearance and taste. Recipe-wise, the two styles are somewhat similar, with the classic Irish stout calling for roasted barley, whereas porter generally gets its color from chocolate malt and black patent malt. Hopswise, the early-addition hops provide some bitterness but usually not all that much in the way of aroma hops.

Porter is a very forgiving beer for beginners. With that in mind, the following recipe is an extract recipe with some grains added for color and flavor. This beer was initially designed for a good friend of mine named Dave Jackson, a connoisseur of single-malt Scotch along with good-quality microbrews and home brews.

Ingredients

3 gallons water

Milled grains:
4 oz. chocolate malt
4 oz. black patent malt
4 oz. 80L Crystal malt

Extract:
6 lbs. amber dried malt extract

Bittering hops:
¾ oz. Chinook hops: boil for 60 minutes

Flavoring hops:
½ oz. Chinook hops: boil for 45 minutes
1 tsp. Irish moss: boil for 15 minutes

Yeast:
1 pack Wyeast British Ale yeast strain 1098

Priming sugar:
⅔ cup corn sugar

Procedure

1. Two days prior to brewing, break the Wyeast smack pack.

2. Heat the water to 155 degrees F and remove from the heat. Add the chocolate, black patent, and crystal malts to a nylon bag and steep for 30 to 45 minutes. Remove the grain bag and drain it into the pot.

3. Bring the wort to a boil. Remove from the heat temporarily.

4. In a second pot, add the dried malt extract. Slowly add 1 to 1½ gallons of the wort to the second pot, stirring constantly until dissolved. Add the rest of the initial wort and bring back to a boil.

5. Add the bittering hops and set a timer to make the next hop addition in 15 minutes.

6. After 15 minutes, add the flavoring hops. Reset the timer for 30 minutes.

7. After 30 minutes, add the Irish moss and continue to boil for 15 minutes.

8. Total boil time is 60 minutes. Remove from the heat, chill to 70 degrees F, add water to equal 5½ gallons of wort, and pitch the yeast.

9. Ferment for 5 days and then rack to your secondary fermentation vessel.

10. After an additional 7 days, bottle and age for 1 to 2 weeks before enjoying.

Pumpkin Ale

By Bart Bullington

Batch size: 5 gallons
Original gravity: 1.052
Final gravity: 1.014
International bitterness units: 45
Alcohol by volume: 5.2 percent

This fun, festive beer celebrates the harvest season. Rich flavors of cinnamon, nutmeg, allspice, and ginger make this session beer a fun drink for autumn holidays. I make it only once a year but always enjoy brewing this favorite.

Ingredients

7½ gallons water

Milled grains:
  1 lb. Crystal malt 60L
  1 lb. Carafoam or Carapils malt

Extract:
  6 lbs. two-row or liquid malt extract

Adjuncts:
  16 oz. pumpkin purée

Bittering hops:
  1 oz. Northern Brewer hops

Finishing and aroma hops:
  3 oz. Fuggle hops, divided

Yeast:
  2 oz. Windsor or Nottingham yeast
  2 oz. Schilling pumpkin pie spice

Procedure

1. Steep the grains in 160- to 165- degree F water for 35 to 40 minutes. If all-grain brewing, steep for 60 minutes.

2. Bring to a boil.

3. For partial grain, add the liquid malt extract when the water is coming to a boil.

4. As the liquid comes to a rolling boil, set a timer for 60 minutes.

5. Add the pumpkin purée and bittering hops.

6. When 20 minutes remain, add 1 oz. Fuggle hops.

7. At end of boil, add 2 oz. Fuggle hops and the pumpkin pie spice.

8. Remove from the heat and stir (aerate) for 20 to 30 minutes.

9. Cool to 70 to 80 degrees F.

10. Transfer into the fermentation vessel.

11. Add the yeast.

12. Ferment for 7 to 10 days at 65 to 69 degrees F.

13. Cold-condition for 3 to 4 days at 34 to 36 degrees F.

Russian Imperial Stout

By Scott Mansfield

Batch size: 5 gallons
Original gravity: 1.092
Final gravity: 1.023
International bitterness units: 73
Alcohol by volume: 9 percent

This Russian Imperial Stout recipe was submitted by Jon Abernathy, founder of and beer blogger with The Brew Site (www.thebrewsite.com). He describes it as a big, fun stout that draws character from both the specialty grains and the molasses. "There are different grades of molasses available that will impart various degrees of flavor," he says, "and I tend to prefer blackstrap in beer because it adds a richer character even though the sugar content is lower."

Abernathy suggests selecting a high alpha-acid hop for the bittering, keeping in mind that it won't make the beer overly hoppy. "The higher amounts of malt will balance out the hops out and vice versa, lending a drinkable balance to the finished beer," he says. "This is also a beer that will age well, so don't hesitate to put it aside."

Ingredients

5 gallons water

Milled grains:
½ lb. black patent malt
½ lb. roasted barley
1 lb. chocolate malt
1 lb. 10L Crystal malt
1 lb. 80L Crystal malt

Extracts and extras:
10 lb. light malt syrup
1 lb. molasses (unsulfured)

Bittering hops:
2 oz. Magnum hops: boil for 60 minutes

Aroma hops:
2 oz. Kent Goldings hops: boil for 15 minutes

Yeast:
Wyeast Irish Ale yeast strain 1084

Priming sugar:
¾ cup corn sugar

Procedure

1. Steep the grains in a nylon mesh bag in the water as it heats to a boil; when the temperature reaches about 180 degrees F, remove the grain bag.

2. Remove the pot from the heat and add the malt extract and molasses, stirring to dissolve thoroughly.

3. Return to the heat, bring to a boil, and add the Magnum hops.

4. After 45 minutes of boiling, add the Kent Goldings hops.

5. After 60 minutes of boiling, remove from the heat.

6. Pour the wort through a strainer into the primary fermentor.

7. Add water to equal 5 gallons.

8. Aerate (stir) and chill/cool and then pitch the yeast.

9. Ferment for 5 to 14 days or until activity stops.

10. Rack to the secondary fermentor and condition for 2 to 3 weeks or longer.

11. Carbonate, bottle, and bottle-condition for at least 3 weeks.

Ales

All-Grain
Recipes

English Pale Ale

By Bart Bullington

Batch size: 5 gallons
Original gravity: 1.056
Final gravity: 1.014
International bitterness units: 58
Alcohol by volume: 5.7 percent

This is an English-style pale ale. Pale ales originated in England with a less aggressive hop finish than those found in America today. This recipe makes a flavorful ale with hints of caramel and toffee and a balanced hop finish.

Ingredients

7½ gallons water

Milled grains:
3 lbs. Crystal 40L Malt
2 lbs. Carafoam or Carapils malt

Extract:
7½ lbs. pale ale malt or liquid malt extract

Bittering hops:
1 oz. Northern Brewer hops

Finishing and aroma hops:
3 oz. Fuggles hops, divided

Yeast:
2 oz. Nottingham yeast

Procedure

1. Steep all of the specialty grains in 160 to 165 degree F water for 30 to 40 minutes.

2. Run the wort off into your brewing vessel. If using liquid malt extract, add it after the transfer.

3. Bring to a rolling boil. When the wort reaches a rolling boil, set a timer for 60 minutes.

4. Add the bittering hops.

5. When 30 minutes remain, add 1 oz. finishing and aroma hops.

6. When 10 minutes remain, add the rest of the finishing and aroma hops.

7. Remove from the heat and stir (aerate) for 10 to 20 minutes.

8. Cool to 70 to 80 degrees F.

9. Add the yeast to the cooled wort and then transfer into the fermentor.

10. Ferment at 65 to 70 degrees F for 10 days.

11. Cold-condition at 34 to 36 degrees F for 3 to 4 days in a finishing/serving vessel or in the same container if using a keg fermentor.

Hefeweizen

By Bart Bullington

Batch size: 5 gallons
Original gravity: 1.052
Final gravity: 1.012
International bitterness units: 28 to 30
Alcohol by volume: 5.25 percent

Hefeweizen, one of the world's oldest beer styles, is cloudy from active yeasts and flavorful, with hints of clove and banana. When visiting Germany, you just might see a nun enjoying a tall glass after Sunday Mass!

Ingredients

7½ gallons water

Milled grains:
4 lbs. white wheat
3 lbs. two-row malt
1 lb. Munich malt

Bittering hops:
1 oz. Perle hops

Finishing and aroma hops:
2 oz. Hallertau hops

Yeast:
2 oz. White Labs' WLP300 Hefeweizen Ale yeast (for a traditional banana and clove nose) or WLP380 Hefeweizen IV Ale yeast (for minimal banana with citrus and apricot notes)

Procedure

1. Steep all of the grains in 162- to 164- degree F water for 60 minutes.

2. Run the wort off into the brewing vessel.

3. Bring to a boil. When the wort reaches a rolling boil, set a timer for 60 minutes.

4. Add the bittering hops.

5. When 15 minutes remain, add the Hallertau hops.

6. When time is up, remove from the heat and stir (aerate) for 20 to 30 minutes.

7. Cool to 65 to 74 degrees F.

8. Add the yeast of your choice to the cooled wort. Transfer to the fermentation vessel.

9. Keep your vessel at 66 to 68 degrees F for 7 to 10 days. At this point, you can serve the beer.

10. Bring the beer to a serving temp of about 38 degrees F.

West Coast Pale Ale

By Bart Bullington

Batch size: 5 gallons
Original gravity: 1.062
Final gravity: 1.014
International bitterness units: 64
Alcohol by volume: 6.2 percent

Popular on the United States' West Coast, this is one of my favorites to brew and drink. Adopted from the British during the shipping trades of the Gold Rush era in California, it has hints of honey and caramel with an aggressive hop flavor.

Ingredients

7½ gallons water

Milled grains:
  7½ lbs. two-row brewer's malt (or liquid malt extract)
  2 lbs. Crystal 30-35L malt
  2 lbs. Carafoam or Carapils malt

Bittering hops:
  1 oz. Chinook hops

Finishing and aroma hops:
  3 oz. Cascade hops, divided

Yeast:
  2 packages White Labs' WLP001 California Ale yeast

Procedure

1. Steep all of the specialty malts in 160- to 165- degree F water for 30 to 45 minutes. If all-grain brewing, steep for 60 minutes.

2. Run the wort off into your brewing vessel. If using liquid malt extract, add it after the transfer.

3. Bring to a rolling boil and then set a timer for 60 minutes.

4. Add the bittering hops.

5. When 20 minutes remain, add 1 oz. of the finishing and aroma hops.

6. When the timer ends, add the rest of the finishing and aroma hops.

7. Remove from the heat and stir (aerate) for 10 to 15 minutes.

8. Cool to 70 to 80 degrees F.

9. Add the yeast.

10. Ferment for 7 days between 64 to 68 degrees F.

11. Cold-condition for 7 days at 34 to 36 degrees F in a finishing/serving vessel or in the same container if using a keg fermentor.

Lagers

Backcountry/ Helles Bock

By Scott Mansfield

Batch size: 6 gallons
Original gravity: 1.070
Final gravity: 1.020
International bitterness units: 28
Alcohol by volume: 6.6 percent

Lager Recipes

Whether you call it a helles-style bock or a blonde bock, this beer is best brewed in winter so it's ready for drinking in early spring, when the back country beckons loudest. This home-brew recipe was originally developed by Brett Thomas. He scaled it up for use at Silver Moon Brewing in Bend, Oregon, where he served as head brewer before becoming brewmaster for Sunriver Brewing Company in Sunriver, Oregon. He describes it as "full bodied and malty, with the hops playing only a supporting role."

Ingredients

2 gallons water

Extracts:
10 lbs. Pilsner malt extract
2 lbs. Munich malt extract

Bittering hops:
½ oz. German Magnum pellets (10 percent AA): boil for 60 minutes
¾ oz. Mt. Hood pellets (5 percent AA): boil for 30 minutes

Aroma hops:
¾ oz. Mt. Hood pellets (5 percent AA)

Yeast:
Wyeast 2278 Czech Pils yeast

Procedure

1. Fill a brewing pot with 2 gallons of water and place on the burner; turn the burner to high.

2. When the water reaches 180 degrees F, stir in the malt extracts and bring to a boil.

3. After 30 minutes of boiling, add the Magnum pellets (the first round of bittering hops).

4. After 60 total minutes, add the Mt. Hood pellets (the second round of bittering hops).

5. After 90 total minutes, turn off the heat and add the aroma hops.

6. Steep for 5 minutes and then pour the wort through a strainer into the primary fermentor.

7. Add water to 6 gallons.

8. Aerate (stir) and chill/cool and then pitch the yeast.

9. Ferment at 55 degrees F for 21 days.

10. Rack to a secondary fermentor and condition at 34 degrees F for at least 8 weeks before bottling.

First Thaw Maibock

By Scott Mansfield

Batch size: 5 gallons
Original gravity: 1.069
Final gravity: 1.019
International bitterness units: 45
Alcohol by volume: 6.5 percent

This traditional Bavarian lager is anything but traditional in the United States. Maibocks are maltier, hoppier, and more alcoholic than what most of us think of when we hear the word "lager." Maibock is a seasonal beer, brewed to be enjoyed during the short Bavarian spring, after the first thaw and before the first blossoms.

To get a crisp, clean flavor from a maibock or any brew that uses a lager yeast, you need to ferment and condition in a place with a steady, cool temperature. Traditionally, this was done in caves. Many modern home brewers have dedicated "lagering" refrigerators, specifically set to the optimum temperature for fermenting with lager yeast. Although this setup makes stellar beers, I have access to a basement and prefer the results of these earth-temperature beers. This recipe calls for 55 degrees F; if you have access to any place with a cool, steady temperature, make this lager and see if you like the results.

Ingredients

2 gallons water

Milled grains:
  1 lb. caramel malt
  1 lb. Munich malt

Extracts:
  7 lbs. Golden Light DME

Bittering hops:
  1½ oz. Perle (US). boil for 60 minutes

Adjuncts:
  1 tsp. gypsum

Aroma hops:
  1 oz. Tettnanger: boil for 10 minutes

Yeast:
  Wyeast 2308 Munich Lager

Procedure

1. Steep the grains in a muslin bag in 2 gallons of 160- to 170- degree F water for 30 minutes.

2. Remove the grains, heat the water to 180 degrees F, stir in the malt extracts, and bring to a boil.

3. Add the bittering hops and gypsum.

4. After 50 minutes of boiling, add the aroma hops.

5. Boil for 10 minutes; turn off the heat.

6. Steep for 5 minutes and then pour the wort through a strainer into a primary fermentor.

7. Add water to 5 gallons.

8. Aerate (stir) and chill to 55 degrees F and then pitch the yeast.

9. Ferment at 55 degrees F for 7 days or until fermentation stops.

10. Rack to a secondary fermentor and condition for 8 weeks (or longer) at a cool, steady temperature before bottling.

Lager

By Bart Bullington

Batch size: 5 gallons
Original gravity: 1.046
Final gravity: 1.014
International bitterness units: 32
Alcohol by volume: 4.19 percent

Lager is the traditional beer. This recipe will result in fuller-flavored golden beer similar to traditional German beers. It has light honey and cracker malts with a light, clean, hoppy finish. This is always a favorite and makes a great session beer.

Ingredients

7½ gallons water

Milled grains:
 1 lb. Munich malt
 4 lbs. two-row brewer's malt (or liquid
  malt extract)

Bittering hops:
 1 oz. Perle hops

Finishing and aroma hops:
 2 oz. Hallertau hops

Yeast:
 2 oz. Saflager S-23 lager yeast

Procedure

1. Steep all of the malts in 160- to 165- degree F water for 30 to 40 minutes. If all-grain brewing, steep for 60 minutes.

2. Heat the mixture to a boil. If using liquid malt extract, add it now. When the wort reaches a rolling boil, set a timer for 60 minutes.

3. Add the bittering hops.

4. When 20 minutes remain, add the finishing and aroma hops.

5. When the timer ends, remove the mixture from the heat and stir (aerate) for 10 to 20 minutes. Cool to 70 to 80 degrees F.

6. Add the yeast.

7. Transfer into a fermentation vessel. Cool to 55 to 60 degrees F.

8. Ferment for 14 to 21 days at 55 to 60 degrees F.

9. Bring the finishing wort temperature down to 33 to 34 degrees F to allow the yeast to go into torpor and to clarify the beer. Cold-condition for a minimum of 14 days in a finishing/serving vessel or in the same container if using a keg fermentor.

Tip: Longer stirring times assist in moving any proteins and hop materials into the center of the kettle.

Tip: A longer fermentation time reduces sulfur tastes.

Vienna Lager

By Bart Bullington

Batch size: 5 gallons
Original gravity: 1.056
Final gravity: 1.014
International bitterness units: 29
Alcohol by volume: 5.2 percent

Popular in Europe, this maltier beer is for the lager drinker interested in something a little richer. It is a deep, amber lager with hints of toffee and dry cracker malt with a balanced hop finish.

Ingredients

7½ gallons water

Milled grains:
1 lb. Vienna malt
1 lb. Caramunich malt
3 oz. chocolate wheat malt
6 lbs. two-row brewer's malt (or light liquid malt extract)

Bittering hops:
1 oz. Magnum hops

Flavor and aroma hops:
1 oz. Perle hops

Finishing and aroma hops:
2 oz. Hallertau hops

Yeast:
2 oz. Saflager S-23 lager yeast

Tip:
Lager yeast performs better in the mid-50s (degrees F).

Procedure

1. Steep all the specialty malts in 160- to 165- degree F water for 30 to 40 minutes. Add the malt extract at the onset of the boil.

2. Heat the mixture to a boil. If using light liquid malt extract, add it now.

3. When the wort reaches a rolling boil, set a timer for 60 minutes.

4. Add the bittering hops and the flavor and aroma hops.

5. When 20 minutes remain, add the finishing and aroma hops.

6. When the timer ends, remove from the heat and stir (aerate) for 10 to 20 minutes.

7. Cool to 70 to 80 degrees F.

8. Add the yeast.

9. Transfer into a fermentation vessel. Cool to 55 to 60 degrees F.

10. Ferment for 14 to 21 days at 55 to 60 degrees F. Tip: Longer fermentation reduces sulfur tastes.

11. Bring the finishing wort temperature down to 33 to 34 degrees F to allow the yeast to go into torpor and to clarify the beer. Cold-condition for a minimum of 14 days in a finishing/serving vessel or in the same container if using a keg fermentor.

Hybrid and Gluten-Free

Halcyon Common

By Scott Mansfield

Batch size: 5 gallons
Original gravity: 1.055
Final gravity: 1.012
International bitterness units: 51.5
Alcohol by volume: 5.6 percent

San Francisco home brewer Eran Dayan developed this recipe after tweaking one for a partial mash of a clone of Anchor Steam Beer. He grows his own Galena hops and makes the grapefruit tincture from scratch on brew night. "I always expect the beer to be conditioned and ready to drink two weeks after bottling but typically find that it is much tastier after three or four," Dayan says. "The resulting grapefruit flavor is subtle, and because the tincture is taken from the rind, it contributes a bitterness that braces the hops with just a hint of fruit aroma."

Note that although the recipe uses a lager yeast, it's fermented at room temperature. This is traditional for California Common/steam beers. Fermenting the lager yeast at a higher temperature adds a distinctive flavor to the beer.

Ingredients

3 gallons water

Milled grains:
1½ lbs. two-row malt
½ lb. special roast malt
¼ lb. Crystal malt 30-37L
¼ lb. flaked barley

Extract:
6 lbs. Pilsen malt extract syrup

Bittering hops:
1 oz. Northern Brewer hops: boil for 60 minutes

Aroma hops:
½ oz. Citra hops: boil for 15 minutes
½ oz. Citra hops: boil for 5 minutes
1 oz. Galena hops: add at the end of boiling

Yeast:
White Labs' WLP810 San Francisco lager yeast

Priming sugar:
¾ cup corn sugar

Extras:
1 cup grapefruit tincture*

Procedure

1. Steep the grains in a grain bag in 3 gallons of 155- to 160- degree F water for 45 minutes.

2. Remove the grains, heat the wort, and stir in the extract just before boiling.

3. When the mixture boils, add the bittering hops and set a timer for 60 minutes.

4. After 45 minutes of boiling, add the first aroma hops.

5. After 55 total minutes of boiling, add the second portion of aroma hops.

6. After 60 minutes of total boiling, turn off the heat and add the Galena hops.

7. Pour the wort through a strainer into the primary fermentor.

8. Add water to equal 5 gallons.

9. Aerate (stir), chill/cool, and then pitch the yeast (add it to the wort).

10. After primary fermentation (usually about 6 days), rack to the carboy.

11. After secondary fermentation (usually 3 weeks after the boil), add the grapefruit tincture to the carboy and rack from the carboy into bottles.

12. Carbonate with priming sugar and bottle-condition for 3 to 4 weeks.

*To make the grapefruit tincture: Peel 1 large grapefruit and submerge the rind in 1 cup of Ketel One Vodka in a jar with an airtight lid. Store out of the direct sunlight until the beer is ready to rack from the primary fermentor to a carboy. During the racking process, pour the tincture directly into the carboy and throw away the rind.

Gluten-Free Honey Lager

By Wendy Wilson

Batch size: 5 gallons
Original gravity: 1.042
Final gravity: 1.008
International bitterness units: 16
Alcohol by volume: 4.5 percent

This gluten-free lager swaps out barley for a type of grass grain called sorghum. Medium to darker varieties of honey blend with the sorghum flavor and combine well with the citrusy- and floral-aroma Cascade and Saaz hops.

Ingredients

4 gallons water

3¾ lbs. Briess' BriesSweet White Sorghum Syrup 45DE High Maltose

1½ lbs. medium to dark honey

½ lb. corn syrup

Bittering hops:
½ oz. Hallertau hops (6 percent AA)

Finishing hops:
¾ oz. Cascade hops
¾ oz. Saaz hops

Yeast:
2 packages dry Wyeast 2206 GF gluten-free yeast

1 cup honey (for priming)

Procedure

1. Bring water to a boil.

2. Add sorghum syrup, honey, and corn syrup to the water, stirring vigorously to dissolve. Bring back to a boil.

3. Add the bittering hops and continue to boil.

4. After 50 minutes, add the Cascade finishing hops.

5. At the very end of the 60-minute boil, add the Saaz finishing hops.

6. Remove from the heat and cool to 55 to 60 degrees Fahrenheit.

7. Transfer to the primary fermentor, fill with cold water to total 5 gallons, oxygenate, and pitch the yeast.

8. Let the mixture ferment for 17 to 18 days at 55 to 60 degrees F.

9. Transfer the wort to a secondary vessel and ferment for at least 14 days at 32 to 35 degrees F.

10. After fermentation completes, prime the beer with 1 cup of honey and bottle.

Sorghum Ale
By Wendy Wilson

Batch size: 5 gallons
Original gravity: 1.055
Final gravity: 1.014
International bitterness units: 33
Alcohol by volume: 5.3 percent

Gluten-Free

Hunting for a gluten-free ale to make at home? Look no further! You won't miss the barley when sipping this sorghum-based ale with a toasted caramel flavor. The Centennial, Cascade, and Amarillo hops add just the right amount of bitterness and aroma.

Ingredients

- 5 gallons water
- 5 lbs. white sorghum malt (base malt)
- 1 lb. white sorghum malt (kilned/toasted malt)
- 1 tsp. amylase enzymes
- 4 lbs. Briess' BriesSweet White Sorghum Syrup 45DE High Maltose

Bittering hops:
- 0.6 oz. Centennial hops (12 percent AA)

Flavoring hops:
- ½ oz. Cascade hops (5 percent AA)

Finishing hops:
- ½ oz. Amarillo hops

Priming sugar:
- ¾ cup corn sugar

Procedure

1. Malt 6 pounds of white sorghum and toast 1 pound of it. Note: To "malt" means to germinate the grain and then dry it in a kiln at a low temperature (122 to 158 degrees F) to about 4 percent moisture. To "toast" the malt, you bring it up to a higher temperature in the kiln (or oven) to 275 degrees F for 1 hour. Be sure to store the malt in a paper bag for a couple of weeks prior to using to allow time for the harsher aromatics to escape.

2. Perform a triple decoction mash: Steep hot water with the malt, pull the liquid from the grain/mash, boil it, return it to the grain/mash, and bring it back up to temperature. Repeat this process three times. The idea is to get as much sugar out of the grain as possible while creating the wort.

3. Heat the mash to 180 degrees F and stir in the amylase enzymes.

4. Collect the wort, add the syrup and the bittering hops, and boil the mixture for 60 minutes.

5. After 30 minutes, add the flavoring hops and continue to boil.

6. At the end of the boil, add the finishing hops.

7. Transfer to the fermentor, oxygenate, and pitch the yeast.

8. Ferment at 70 degrees F.

9. After fermentation completes, prime the beer with corn sugar and bottle.

Food Recipes

Sure, you could drink or give away every bottle of your home-brewed bounty—and you should do that with most of your beer—but why not use some of your hard-won brews in some culinary creations, too? Beer's trademark flavor suits a wide variety of dishes, from dinner to dessert, and your level of craftsmanship is just going to take recipes to the next level.

We've curated a number of dishes here that will feature your delicious home-brews. Keep in mind that any experimental flavors you've put into your beer will also come through in your cooking. If you've brewed a fruit-forward hefeweizen or American wheat ale, give the Hefeweizen Chicken Tacos with Avocado Salsa or Apricot Pecan Tart a try. The fruity flavors will bring another flavor dimension to these foods.

Don't be discouraged from trying some of these recipes even if you don't have the exact beer style that they call for, either. For example, the Chocolate Stout Pretzel Pie (how good does that sound?) is best with a stout or a porter, but if you don't have any on hand, substitute an amber or a brown ale. It's still going to be delicious. Of course, don't use a radically different beer style, like an IPA, though—those citrusy, hoppy notes are not a natural marriage with rich chocolate and salty pretzels. Or are they? Take home brewing's spirit of experimentation into the kitchen with you!

On to the recipes! Now you can drink your beer and eat it, too.

Appetizer Recipes

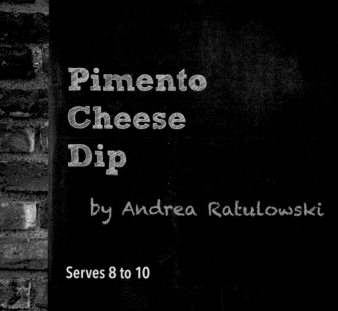

Pimento Cheese Dip

by Andrea Ratulowski

Serves 8 to 10

This offers a twist on cheese dip using pimentos to provide color and a sweet bite, while the IPA brings a tartness that highlights the sharp Cheddar and horseradish. This cheese dip can be served cold or heated just before serving.

Ingredients

- ½ cup IPA
- 8 oz. cream cheese
- 8 oz. block of sharp Cheddar cheese, shredded
- 2 Tbsp. prepared horseradish
- 2 Tbsp. Dijon mustard
- ½ tsp. salt
- ½ tsp. garlic powder
- ½ tsp. onion powder
- 8 oz. chopped pimentos, drained and with all excess liquid removed
- 2 green onions, sliced thinly

Procedure

1. In a food processor, combine the IPA, cheeses, horseradish, mustard, and seasonings. Blend until smooth and thickened.

2. Transfer the mixture to a large mixing bowl. Add the pimentos and green onions. Gently stir until everything becomes well-combined.

3. Cover and refrigerate for at least 5 hours before serving. This allows the mixture to firm up and for all of the flavors to combine.

4. **Optional:** If you want to serve this warm, preheat the oven to 400 degrees Fahrenheit. (Baking it will prevent the dip from turning into mush.) Transfer the mixture to an oven-safe baking dish. Bake for about 15 minutes or until the mixture bubbles.

Tip

This dish can be served with pretzels, veggies, and all manner of crackers. It's also great as a burger topping or on grilled-cheese sandwiches!

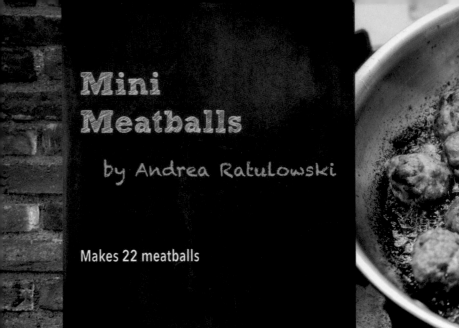

Mini Meatballs

by Andrea Ratulowski

Makes 22 meatballs

These bite-sized meatballs are perfect for game day or your next potluck! They go well with the sweet and spicy barbecue sauce on page 183 that highlights the freshness of a wheat beer. You can simmer the meatballs in the sauce, or you can serve the sauce on the side.

Ingredients

1 lb. (80 percent lean, 20 percent fat) ground beef

1 egg

½ Tbsp. Worcestershire sauce

¼ cup breadcrumbs

½ tsp. salt

1 tsp. ground black pepper

1 tsp. garlic powder

1 tsp. onion powder

1 tsp. chili powder

1 Tbsp. olive oil or other cooking oil

Procedure

1. In a large mixing bowl, combine all of the ingredients by hand except for the oil.

2. Using a tablespoon, scoop out the mixture and shape it into mini meatballs. Repeat until all of the mixture is used. You should end up with about 22 meatballs.

3. Sauté: In a large skillet, heat the oil over medium-high heat. Place the meatballs in the skillet and cook on each side for about 5 minutes or until the meatballs are browned and cooked all the way through. Remove from the heat and set aside.

-or-

Bake: Preheat the oven to 400 degrees F. Place the meatballs on a cookie sheet greased with the oil. Bake for about 15 minutes or until the meatballs are cooked through. Remove from the heat and set aside.

Appetizer Recipes

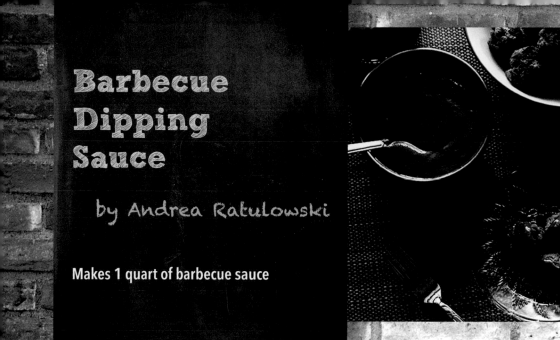

Barbecue Dipping Sauce

by Andrea Ratulowski

Makes 1 quart of barbecue sauce

Ingredients

1 Tbsp. olive oil or cooking oil

1 red pepper, cut into chunks

2 roasted green chiles, seeds removed and cut into chunks

2 garlic cloves

1 medium-sized Vidalia or sweet onion, cut into chunks

1 tsp. salt

1 tsp. chili powder

1 tsp. ground black pepper

1 tsp. garlic powder

1 tsp. smoked paprika

12 oz. wheat beer

1 cup ketchup

½ cup yellow mustard

¼ cup blackstrap molasses

2 Tbsp. Worcestershire sauce

2 Tbsp. apple cider vinegar

Procedure

1. In a large saucepan, heat the oil over medium-high heat. Add the chopped pepper, chiles, garlic, and onion. Stir until all of the vegetables are covered in oil.

2. Add all of the seasonings and stir. Continue to cook the vegetables until they start to soften—about 15 minutes.

3. Add the wheat beer, ketchup, mustard, molasses, Worcestershire sauce, and apple cider vinegar and stir. Bring to a simmer; simmer for about 30 minutes.

4. Turn off the heat and transfer the contents to a blender. Blend on high until the sauce becomes smooth and creamy. (Optional: you can use an immersion blender.) Start at a low speed, and gradually work up to a higher speed. Again, blend until the sauce becomes smooth and creamy.

5. Transfer the sauce back to the saucepan and bring to a simmer. Simmer for about 10 minutes and then remove from the heat. Transfer the sauce to a heatproof container and either use right away or store until ready. Leftover sauce can be saved or frozen.

To Serve

Both the meatballs on page 182 and the sauce can be made the day before serving. To serve, heat the meatballs in the sauce and transfer to a bowl. You also can heat them separately by warming the meatballs up in a 400-degree Fahrenheit oven for about 10 minutes and heating the sauce in a pot until simmering. Serve each separately, and allow your guests to add the sauce.

Bread Recipes

Italian-ish Beer Bread

by Sharon Kebschull Barrett

Makes 1 large loaf, 2 smaller loaves, or 8-10 rolls

For chewy loaves of bread, 5-minute, no-knead bread recipes work well with beer replacing the water. But sometimes a lighter, more tender loaf hits the spot, and this recipe, made with a flavorful beer, works perfectly for big loaves as well as hoagie-sized rolls. Better yet, it lends itself to all sorts of experimentation, from the type of beer to multiple add-ins. It's delicious made with hefeweizen, a fruity wheat beer, even a milk stout—anything but a very hoppy beer that can create a bitter aftertaste in the bread. Add more flavor with herbs such as rosemary, thyme, or savory, or try cubes of cheese or some crumbled bacon and cheese together.

Ingredients

3½ cups bread flour, more if needed

2 tsp. instant yeast

1 tsp. fine sea salt

Optional dough add-ins:
 1 to 2 Tbsp. minced rosemary, thyme or, savory or a combination of herbs; and/or 1¼ cups diced cheese, such as Swiss, provolone, fontina, or Cheddar; and/or 1 cup crumbled cooked bacon or diced ham

3 Tbsp. olive oil

2 Tbsp. honey

12 oz. beer at room temperature or warmed to about 110 degrees F

1 egg white beaten with 2 tsp. water

Optional topping:
 1 Tbsp. poppy or white or black sesame seeds

Procedure

1. In a large bowl, thoroughly whisk together flour, yeast and salt; if using herbs, whisk them in now. Add oil, honey, and beer. Stir with a spatula until well mixed.

2. If using a stand mixer, knead using the dough hook for 4 minutes on medium speed (or the manufacturer's recommended speed). If making by hand, turn the dough onto a lightly floured surface and knead for 8 to 10 minutes or until the dough becomes smooth and elastic. If the dough is too sticky to knead by hand, add up to ¼ cup more flour. Knead in other additions, such as cheese or bacon, at the end of the kneading.

3. Cover the dough with lightly greased plastic wrap or a damp towel and let rise until doubled—about 1 hour.

4. Gently flatten the dough and divide into thirds. Roll each piece under your hands into a 16-inch strand. Braid strands together on a parchment paper-lined or greased baking sheet, pinching ends together and tucking them under.

5. Cover and let rise about 30 minutes until nearly doubled. Preheat the oven to 375 degrees F.

6. When the dough is ready, brush lightly with egg white and sprinkle with seeds, if using. Bake for 25 to 30 minutes until golden-brown (if making rolls, reduce baking by 5 to 10 minutes).

Beer-Bacon Cornbread

by Sharon Kebschull Barrett

**Makes 1 pan of cornbread
(about 8 servings)**

Take traditional Southern cornbread in a different direction with beer. A fairly strong ale or lager works well here to balance the strong bacon. Take it a step further by sprinkling grated Cheddar over the top during the last 5 minutes of baking. You could even serve it with honey butter for a sweet-salty combination. If you don't have a cast-iron skillet, bake in a cake tin. Grease the bottom and sides with the bacon fat and heat the cake tin in the oven while the oven preheats.

Ingredients

12 slices bacon (about 8 oz., or more if desired), chopped

1½ cups yellow cornmeal, preferably stone-ground

½ cup all-purpose flour, preferably unbleached

½ tsp. fine sea salt

2 tsp. sugar

½ tsp. baking powder

¼ tsp. baking soda

1 large egg

¾ cup beer

¾ cup buttermilk (shake well before using)

Procedure

1. Preheat the oven to 450 degrees Fahrenheit. In a 9-inch cast-iron skillet, cook bacon over medium heat until crisp. Drain on paper towels.

2. Pour out bacon fat from the pan; add ¼ cup back to the pan, and discard the rest or chill to use another time. Keep the pan on low heat while you make the batter.

3. In a medium bowl, whisk together cornmeal, flour, salt, sugar, baking powder, and baking soda.

4. In a separate bowl, whisk together egg, beer, and buttermilk; stir in the cornmeal mixture just until blended. Fold in the cooked bacon. Swirl the skillet lightly to distribute the bacon fat.

5. Carefully spread the batter into the hot skillet (it might spatter), and transfer the skillet to the oven. Bake 20 to 25 minutes until golden and firm. Serve immediately.

Main Dishes

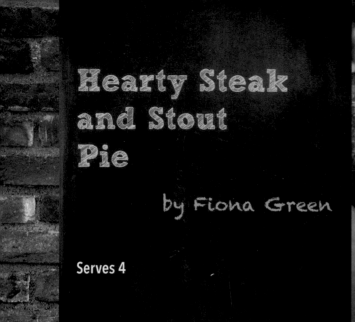

Hearty Steak and Stout Pie

by Fiona Green

Serves 4

I grew up in Scotland, where steak pie is a very popular meal. It's not surprising that this dish is so well-liked. The combination of moist, tender chunks of steak; rich gravy; and light puff pastry guarantees a tasty meal that will satisfy even the biggest appetite. This recipe uses carrots, potatoes, and parsnips; feel free to use other vegetables.

Ingredients

2 Tbsp. olive oil

1½ lb. beef stew meat

1 medium onion, chopped

2 medium potatoes, diced

2 medium carrots, sliced

1 parsnip, sliced

1 14-oz. can diced tomatoes

2 cups stout beer

1 Tbsp. Worcestershire sauce

1 Tbsp. mustard

1 Tbsp. cocoa powder

1 Tbsp. fresh parsley

1 Tbsp. dried thyme

salt and pepper to taste

1 puff pastry sheet (from a box containing 1.1 lbs.)

1 egg, beaten

Procedure

1. In a large pan, heat the olive oil and brown the meat for 4 to 5 minutes. Add the onion. Cook for 2 minutes.

2. Add the potatoes, carrots, and parsnip. Continue cooking for 5 minutes, and then add the tomatoes, stout, Worcestershire sauce, mustard, cocoa powder, and herbs.

3. Let the liquid come to a boil. Cover the pan, reduce the heat, and simmer for 1½ to 2 hours. Check every 30 minutes to make sure that sufficient liquid remains in the pan. If not, add a little more stout–up to ½ cup.

4. When the meat becomes tender, remove it from the heat and leave it at room temperature for approximately 10 minutes. Preheat the oven to 375 degrees F.

5. Pour the stew into a 1-quart casserole dish. Roll out the puff pastry to about 1 inch wider than the dish and place it on top to cover the stew.

6. Brush with the beaten egg and cook on the lowest rack of the oven for approximately 20 minutes or until the pastry appears golden-brown. If the crust browns too quickly, cover it lightly with foil. Serve with fresh peas or mixed vegetables.

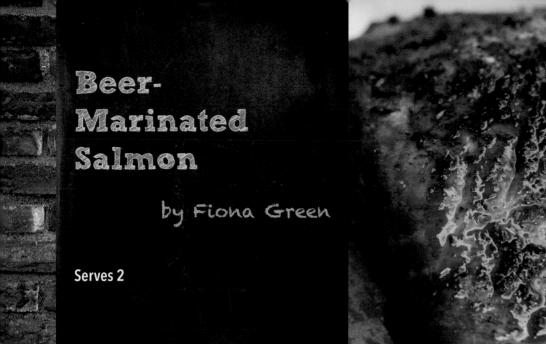

Beer-Marinated Salmon

by Fiona Green

Serves 2

Grilled salmon gets a delicious upgrade in this recipe that features fresh fillets soaked in a smoky, garlicky pale-ale marinade before being oven-baked or grilled to perfection on a cedar plank. Consider preparing a couple of extra fillets to add to a fresh green salad the next day.

Ingredients

2 5-oz. salmon fillets

Blackening Rub

1 Tbsp. paprika

1 tsp. salt

2 tsp. ground cumin

½ tsp. dried parsley

2 tsp. ground black pepper

½ tsp. mustard powder

½ tsp. ground chipotle chile pepper

Marinade

½ cup pale ale plus 1 cup for soaking the cedar plank

¼ cup soy sauce

2 Tbsp. mustard

2 tsp. minced garlic

2 Tbsp. lime juice

1 tsp. liquid smoke

1 tsp. coconut vinegar (apple cider vinegar can be used)

1 tsp. cracked black pepper

salt to taste

Glaze

2 Tbsp. honey or agave syrup

Procedure

1. Prepare the blackening rub by mixing together all of the ingredients. Set aside in a jar for later use.

2. Rinse the salmon, place it in a sealed plastic bag with the marinade ingredients, mix together, and refrigerate for about 4 hours.

3. Grill: Soak the cedar plank in 1 cup beer while the salmon marinates. Remove the plank from the beer and allow it to air-dry. Brush one side of the plank with olive oil to prevent the fish from sticking. Place the salmon on the cedar plank, baste with honey, and add the blackening rub. Cook on the grill over indirect medium-high heat for 20 to 30 minutes depending on the thickness of the fish.

-or-

Bake. Preheat the oven to 375 degrees F. Wrap the salmon in foil and bake for 20 minutes. Remove the fish from the oven, baste with honey, and sprinkle the blackening rub on top. Return to the oven for 10 minutes uncovered.

4. Serve with pasta or vegetable risotto.

Hefeweizen Chicken Tacos with Avocado Salsa

by Jennifer Mackenzie

Serves 4

Hefeweizen's characteristic light taste with citrus notes complements the mild, fragrant spices in this braised chicken-taco filling. You can add traditional taco toppings such as lettuce, cheese, and sour cream if you prefer, although the simplicity of these tacos does seem to shine without much else.

Ingredients

2 lbs. skinless, bone-in chicken thighs (about 8)

salt and freshly ground black pepper to taste

2 Tbsp. vegetable oil

1 small onion, thinly sliced

2 garlic cloves, minced

1 jalapeño pepper, minced

2 tsp. chili powder

½ tsp. ground cumin

pinch ground cinnamon

12 oz. Hefeweizen or other wheat beer

1 avocado

½ lime, juiced

hot pepper sauce

8 to 12 small corn or flour tortillas

Tip

You can prepare the chicken and sauce ahead of time. Braise the chicken, shred it, and let it cool. Cool the sauce separately and then combine it with the chicken. Cover and refrigerate for up to 2 days. Reheat in a skillet over medium heat, stirring often, until heated through.

For a bolder-flavored filling, increase the chili powder to 1 Tbsp. or add a pinch up to ¼ tsp. of ground chipotle chile pepper.

Procedure

1. Season the chicken with salt and pepper. In a large skillet, heat the oil over medium-high heat. Brown the chicken, turning once, for 2 to 3 minutes per side or until golden-brown. Transfer to a bowl.

2. Reduce the heat to medium-low. Sauté the onion for 3 minutes or until starting to soften. Add the garlic, jalapeño, chili powder, cumin, and cinnamon and sauté for 2 minutes or until the onion becomes soft.

3. Add the hefeweizen, increase the heat to high, and bring to a boil, stirring and scraping up the brown bits stuck to the pan.

4. Return the chicken and any accumulated juices to the pan. Reduce the heat to medium-low, cover, and simmer for about 30 minutes, flipping the chicken pieces halfway through cooking or until the chicken is very tender. Remove from the heat.

5. Using a slotted spoon, transfer the chicken to a bowl and let cool slightly. Set the pan of sauce aside. Remove the bones from the chicken and shred the meat. Return the chicken to the sauce and bring to a simmer over medium heat, stirring often. Season to taste with salt and pepper. Reduce the heat to low and keep hot.

6. Dice the avocado and combine it in a bowl with the lime juice, salt, and hot pepper sauce to taste.

7. Warm the tortillas in a dry skillet over medium heat, stacking in a piece of foil to keep warm, or warm in the oven according to package directions.

8. Spoon the chicken in sauce into warm tortillas and top with the avocado salsa.

Stout-Braised Mussels with Caramelized Onions

by Jennifer Mackenzie

Serves 2

Just a few bold ingredients give you plenty of punch in this dish that's fit to be served at even the finest gastropub. The depth of flavor from the stout holds up well to the mussels without overpowering them and is accented nicely by the caramelized onions. Serve crusty baguette or rolls alongside to soak up the delicious juices.

Ingredients

2 Tbsp. butter

2 onions, thinly sliced

½ tsp. finely chopped fresh rosemary

¼ tsp. salt

freshly ground pepper to taste

2 lbs. fresh mussels

12 oz. stout

1 Tbsp. freshly squeezed lemon juice

Tips

You can double the recipe to make four servings. Just make sure to use a very large pot that can fit the mussels without crowding, and shake the pot gently while they cook to allow them to steam evenly.

For easy entertaining, prepare the onions through step 1 up to 8 hours ahead. Cover the pot and set aside at room temperature until ready to cook the mussels. Reheat the onions over medium heat until sizzling before proceeding with step 2.

Procedure

1. In a large pot, melt the butter over medium-high heat. Sauté the onions for 2 minutes or until they start to wilt. Reduce the heat to low, cover, and cook, stirring occasionally, for about 20 minutes or until the onions start to turn golden.

2. Stir in the rosemary, salt, and pepper to taste. Cook, covered, stirring often, for about 10 minutes or until the onions are very soft and golden. Uncover and cook, stirring, for 10 minutes or until well caramelized.

3. Meanwhile, rinse the mussels, remove the beards, and scrub to remove any grit, if necessary. Tap any open mussels and discard those that do not close.

4. Pour the stout into the pot with the onions and increase the heat to high. Bring to a boil, stirring and scraping up any brown bits stuck to the pot.

5. Add the mussels, cover, and boil for 5 to 8 minutes or until they have opened. Discard any mussels that do not open.

6. Using a slotted spoon, portion the mussels into warmed serving bowls. Stir lemon juice into the broth, and spoon the caramelized onions and broth over the mussels.

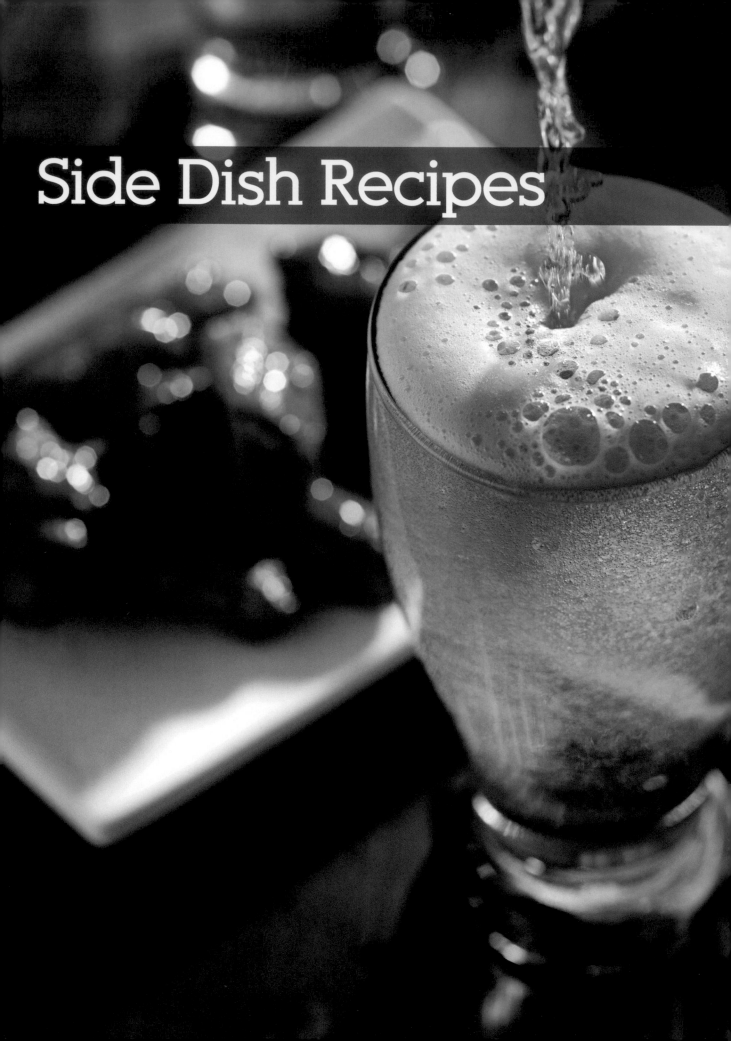

Side Dish Recipes

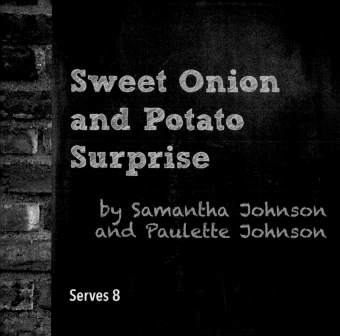

Sweet Onion and Potato Surprise

by Samantha Johnson and Paulette Johnson

Serves 8

Thick, creamy, and hearty, this veggie side dish brings out the peerless taste and texture of sweet potatoes and onions while introducing brown ale, brown sugar, and bacon to kick up the flavor. This recipe feeds a crowd, so invite your friends and dig in!

Ingredients

1 large Vidalia or other sweet onion, chopped
3 Tbsp. butter
2 Tbsp. plus ⅓ cup brown sugar
4 large sweet potatoes, peeled and chopped
¾ cup brown ale
½ tsp. cinnamon
¼ tsp. nutmeg
1 cup cream
10 bacon slices, cooked and chopped
freshly ground black pepper to taste (optional)

Procedure

1. In a large skillet, combine onion, butter, and 2 Tbsp. brown sugar. Cook for approximately 10 minutes over medium-high heat until brown and soft.

2. In a saucepan, boil the sweet potatoes until fork-tender. Drain the water, then lightly mash.

3. Add ale to the skillet, then cook 3 to 5 minutes until it reduces.

4. Add sweet potatoes, cinnamon, nutmeg, cream, and the remaining ⅓ cup of brown sugar to the skillet. Stir to combine. Continue to heat until the mixture is thoroughly heated.

5. Remove from the heat and stir in the bacon. Add pepper if desired.

Funky Chunky Applesauce

by Samantha Johnson
and Paulette Johnson

Serves 6 to 8

Got apples? Cook up festively fruity fun with this chunky-style applesauce. Raisins, cloves, and cinnamon set the stage to highlight your favorite fruit beer, and the simple steps make recipe prep a breeze.

Ingredients

8 Granny Smith apples: 5 chopped and 3 grated
1 cup raisins
¾ cup fruit beer
½ cup brown sugar
¼ cup water
½ tsp. cinnamon
⅛ tsp. ground cloves

Procedure

1. Add ingredients to a large saucepan, reserving only the grated apples.

2. Cook over medium-high heat until the apples are soft and the liquid has reduced—about 20 minutes.

3. Add the grated apples and stir.

Dessert Recipes

Apple Lager Cake with Beer-Caramel Sauce

by Patricia Lehnhardt

Serves 8 to 10

Rich beer-flavored cake layered with spicy apples emulates the taste of autumn. The tartness of the lager balances the sweetness of the caramel to add just the right finishing flavor combination.

Batter

- 12 oz. lager
- ½ cup butter
- ½ cup sugar
- 4 large eggs
- ½ cup canola oil
- 2½ cups cake flour
- ½ tsp. fine sea salt
- 1 Tbsp. baking powder
- 1 Tbsp. raw sugar crystals

Apple Layer

- 3 large Granny Smith apples (1½ lbs.), peeled and sliced ¼-inch thick
- 1 lemon, juiced
- ¼ cup brown sugar
- 1 tsp. ground cinnamon

Beer-Caramel Sauce

- 1 cup sugar
- 2 Tbsp. light corn syrup
- ½ cup lager
- 3 Tbsp. butter
- 1 tsp. sea salt

In a medium saucepan, combine sugar, corn syrup, and lager. Bring to a boil, stirring until the sugar dissolves. Cook until the mixture becomes amber in color and reaches 230 degrees F when measured with a candy thermometer. Remove from the heat and stir in the butter and salt. Cool.

Procedure

1. Preheat the oven to 350 degrees F. Spray a 9 × 2½-inch springform pan with nonstick spray.

2. In a large saucepan over high heat, cook the beer (it will foam up initially) for 8 to 10 minutes to reduce to ½ cup. Cool.

3. In the large bowl of a stand mixer, cream the butter and sugar until fluffy–about 5 minutes. Beat in the eggs one at a time, beating for 1 minute after each.

4. In a separate bowl, combine the oil and reduced beer.

5. In another bowl, sift together the flour, salt, and baking powder.

6. With the mixer on low speed, beat in one-third of the dry ingredients and then one-half of the wet. Add another third of the dry ingredients and then the remaining oil and beer mixture. Finally, add the remaining flour mixture, beating just until thoroughly combined.

7. In a large bowl, toss together the apples, lemon juice, brown sugar, and cinnamon to evenly coat the apple slices.

8. Spread one-third of the batter in the bottom of the prepared springform pan. Layer one-third of the apples evenly on top of the batter. Repeat these layers two times, ending with apples. Sprinkle with the sugar crystals.

9. Bake for 65 to 70 minutes or until a toothpick comes out clean when inserted into the center of the cake.

10. Cool on a rack. Serve with a drizzle of beer-caramel sauce.

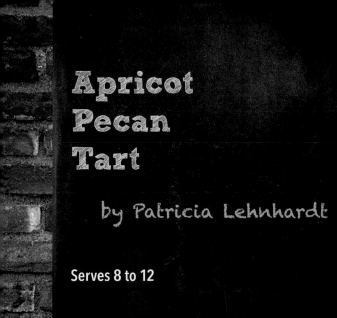

Apricot Pecan Tart

by Patricia Lehnhardt

Serves 8 to 12

In this luscious shortbread dessert, beer enhances the flavor of sweet, tart apricots. It's perfect with afternoon tea or as a sweet finish for a backyard barbecue.

Filling

6 oz. dried apricots, quartered
12 oz. wheat beer
¾ cup sugar

Crust

1½ cups all-purpose flour
¼ cup brown sugar
½ cup finely chopped pecans
¼ tsp. fine sea salt
¾ cup butter, softened
⅓ cup coarsely chopped pecans

Filling Procedure

1. Combine apricots and beer in a medium saucepan. Bring to a boil. Turn off the heat, cover, and rehydrate for 1 hour.

2. Add sugar and bring to a boil, stirring until sugar dissolves. Cook at a gentle boil until thickened and sticky–25 to 30 minutes. It should read 212 degrees F on a candy thermometer. Cool.

Crust Procedure

1. Preheat the oven to 350 degrees F. Coat an 8-inch deep tart pan with a removable bottom with oil.

2. In a medium bowl, combine flour, sugar, pecans, and salt. Mix in the butter until it forms a crumbly dough. Reserve 1 cup.

3. Press the remaining dough into the tart pan, building up the sides to about 1 inch.

4. Spread the apricot filling over the crust and top with the reserved crumbs and pecans.

5. Bake 45 to 50 minutes until golden-brown. Cool on a rack for 15 minutes. Remove the tart from the pan and cool completely.

Chocolate Stout Pretzel Pie

by Patricia Lehnhardt

Serves 8

Beer, chocolate, and pretzels make a great combination that tastes even better in this brownie-like pie. It's great for snacking or completing a beer-infused banquet. The bitterness of the stout and the saltiness of the pretzels tone down the sweetness.

Crust

2 cups broken pretzel sticks
2 Tbsp. brown sugar
¼ cup all-purpose flour
5 Tbsp. melted butter

Filling

4 Tbsp. butter
4 oz. bittersweet chocolate, chopped
2 large eggs
½ cup sugar
½ cup stout
½ cup flour
pinch of fine sea salt
1 tsp. confectioner's sugar for dusting

Crust Procedure

1. In a food processor, combine pretzels, brown sugar, and flour. Process until finely ground. Add butter and process until thoroughly combined and moist.

2. Transfer mixture to a 9-inch standard pie plate. Press into the bottom and sides, adding a rim on top.

Filling Procedure

1. Preheat the oven to 375 degrees F.

2. Melt butter and chocolate together in a double boiler or in the microwave. Cool.

3. In a medium bowl, use an electric hand mixer to beat the eggs and sugar until light-colored and fluffy. Add the stout, flour, and salt and beat until smooth. Add the chocolate and butter mixture and beat until well combined. Pour into the crust.

4. Bake 30 to 35 minutes until set and the crust looks golden. Cool on a rack. Dust with confectioner's sugar if desired.

Glossary

aerate: to add oxygen by stirring the wort (unfermented beer) during brewing. This is done after cooling and just before fermentation, as yeast requires oxygen to ferment completely.

all-grain brewing: This more advanced method of brewing uses malted grains, not extracts.

alpha acids or AA: the chemical compounds that produce bitterness in beer; shown as a percentage in hops.

batch sparge: to drain the wort completely from the mash.

bottle condition: a process during which yeast naturally carbonates beer after fermentation is complete.

carboy: a large, cylindrical jug of 3 to 15 gallons in size, used for secondary fermentation. Most home brewers use the 5-gallon size.

cold condition: to chill the beer to clear it without the use of fining agents.

DME: dry malt extract.

fermentation: During brewing, this process converts sugar to alcohol. It occurs via yeast and bacteria.

fermenter: the person doing the fermenting.

fermentor: the vessel in which fermentation occurs.

fining agent: a compound added to beer during boiling or later that rapidly clears the beer.

fly sparge (or continuous sparge): to add water at the same slow rate at which the wort is drained.

hops: the female flowers of the hop plant. They provide flavor to beer.

lautering: the process of separating the wort from the mash.

mash: *verb* – to combine grains with water and heat the mixture, breaking down the starch in the grains into sugars and producing wort; *noun* – the heated grains, which are separated from the water.

mash tun: a vessel for mashing.

priming: to add sugar-water to a batch of beer just before bottling it.

racking: to transfer the beer to a second fermentor without disturbing the sediments or exposing it to air.

secondary fermentation: the process of aging and maturing beer, also called *conditioning*; see *bottle condition* and *cold condition*.

session beer: Typically lower in alcohol (5 percent or lower), this beer can be consumed in larger quantities.

sparge: to rinse the mashed grains with hot water at the end of mashing.

wort: the malty liquid extracted from the mashing process during beer brewing. This word translates to "unfermented beer" in German.

Resources

Books

Bostwick, William and Jessi Rymill. *Beer Craft.*
Emmaus, PA: Rodale Books, 2011.

Brier, Robert M. and Hoyt Hobbs. *Daily Life
of the Ancient Egyptians.* Westport, CT:
Greenwood Publishing Group, 2008.

Calagione, Sam. *Extreme Brewing: An
Introduction to Brewing Craft Beer at Home.*
Beverly, MA: Quarry Books, 2012.

Goldfarb, Aaron and Michael Zambotti. *Drunk
Drinking.* Amazon Digital Services, Inc.

Jones, David M. *The Inca World: Ancient People
and Places.* London: Anness Publishing, 2010.

Papazian, Charlie. *The Complete Joy of
Homebrewing,* 3rd edition. New York:
HarperResource, 2003.

Breweries

The Bruery
Placentia, CA
www.thebruery.com

Dogfish Head Craft Brewed Ales
Milton, DE (brewery) and Rehoboth Beach, DE
(brewpub)
www.dogfish.com

The Olde Mecklenburg Brewery
Charlotte, NC
www.oldemeckbrew.com

Sunriver Brewing Company
Sunriver, OR
www.sunriverbrewingcompany.com

Two Shy Brewing
Roseburg, OR
www.twoshybrewing.com

Home-Brew Supply Stores

Adventures in Homebrewing
www.homebrewing.org
313-277-2739
Retail sites in Taylor and Ann Arbor, MI

Label Peelers
http://labelpeelers.com
330-678-6400
Retail site in Kent, OH

Midwest Supplies
www.midwestsupplies.com
888-449-2739
Retail site in Minneapolis, MN

MoreBeer!
www.morebeer.com
800-600-0033
Retail sites in Concord, Los Altos, and
Riverside, CA

Northern Brewer Homebrew Supply

www.northernbrewer.com

800-681-2739

Retail sites in Minneapolis and St. Paul, MN, and Milwaukee, WI

O'Shea Brewing Company

www.osheabrewing.com

949-364-4440

Retail site in Laguna Niguel, CA

Rebel Brewer

www.rebelbrewer.com

615-859-2188

Retail site in Goodlettsville, TN

Seven Bridges Cooperative (Organic Brewing)

www.breworganic.com

800-768-4409

Retail site in Santa Cruz, CA

Online Tools

Hops Comparison Chart

Brew Your Own

https://byo.com

Click on "Resource Guide" and then "Hop Chart."

Priming Sugar Calculator

Northern Brewer

www.northernbrewer.com

Click on "Learn," then "Resources," and then "Priming Sugar Calculator" from the list on the left-hand side.

Recipe Calculators

Brewer's Friend

www.brewersfriend.com

Click on "Beer Recipe Builder."

TastyBrew

www.tastybrew.com/calculators/recipe.html

Click on "Calculators" and then "Complete Recipe Calculation."

Organizations

American Homebrewers Association

www.homebrewersassociation.org

Cooperative Extension System

nifa.usda.gov/extension

German Beer Institute

www.germanbeerinstitute.com

Websites

BeerAdvocate

www.beeradvocate.com

The Brew Site

www.thebrewsite.com

Craft Beer

www.craftbeer.com

Fermentedly Challenged

www.fermentedlychallenged.com

Index

Note: Recipes are highlighted in **bold** typeface.

Photos

Front cover: Valentyn Volkov/Shutterstock

Back cover: Dorota Zietak/Shutterstock

Spine: microvector/Shutterstock

Title page: Igors Rusakovs/Shutterstock

Background, chapter openers: Ruggiero Scardigno/Shutterstock

Background, sidebars: mexrix/Shutterstock

Shutterstock:
ABBYDOG, 58; Active branding, 197 (bottom); Adwo, 114; Africa Studio, 65 (inset); Tobias Arhelger, 44 (bottom); Stepan Bormotov, 94 (top); Heike Brauer, 33; Alexander Chaikin, 11; Clear_Pictures, 80; Ysbrand Cosijn, 171; Paul Cowan, 41 (bottom); Steve Cukrov, 121; Peter Dedeurwaerder, 15; de2marco, 181 (bottom); francesco de marco, 144; design56, 127; serg_dibrova, 167 (bottom); Digieva, 9 (top); Claudio Divisia, 172; Christian Draghici, 178; EnolaBrain81, 131 (top); ffolas, 176 (top); fotorince, 86, 87; freeskyline, 110; gresei, 156; Chris Hellyar, 42 (top); Brent Hofacker, 151, 163 (top), 164, 169; Oliver Hoffmann, 165, 167 (top); Steve Holderfield, 45; Anna Hoychuk, 30; ifong, 25; inxti, 27; Jag_cz, 112; Petr Jilek, 134; Matt Jordan, 40 (bottom), 62 (top), 106, 109; Marta Jonina, 10; Evgeny Karandaev, 145; Kasza, 71; Kirill Z, 72, 74 (top), 76, 126; Kishivan, 12; Nadiia Korol, 74 (bottom); Dan Kosmayer, 116 (bottom left); Patryk Kosmider, 81 (top); KPG_Payless, 57; A and I Kruk, 175; Anna Kucherova, 30 (bottom); Kyrien, 73 (top); Linda Z., 90; Alexlukin, 131 (bottom); mangpoor2004, 2-3; Mariyana M, 40 (top); matin, 10 (inset); MaxyM, 26, 68, 147, 148; Olga Miltsova, 116 (bottom right); AlekseyMorosov, 146; Mtsaride, 75 (top), 160; Alik Mulikov, 77 (bottom); NatashaPhoto, 159 (top); Dmitry Naumov, 79 (bottom); Maks Narodenko, 161; Miro Novak, 103; oksana2010, 41 (top); Paket, 150; pandapaw, 157 (top); Andrey_Popov, 122; Glenn Price, 75 (bottom), 78 (top), 84 (top); PSD photography, 22; Aaron Rayburn, 142; Joshua Resnick, 70, 192; ronstik, 155; Barbara Rozman, 5, 193 (bottom); Josep M Penalver Rufas, 21; S_Photo, 32; Dmitriy Saveliev, 39 (top); Sayanjo65, 177; Scruggelgreen, 168; SeDemi, 14; Yuriy Seleznev, 24; Shebeko, 174; Dima Sobko, 93; somchaij, 84 (bottom), 118; Alex Standiford, 77 (top); STILLFX, 16; stockcreations, 180; stockphoto-graf, 78 (bottom), 81 (bottom); Subbotina Anna, 127; sunabesyou, 117; Mariusz Szczygiel, 106; Timmary, 194 (top); Wouter Tolenaars, 170; Denise Torres, 173; Julia Tsokur, 30 (top), 163 (bottom); TunedIn by Westend61, 46; udra11, 4; marekuliasz, 29, 129 (bottom); Viktor1, 186 (bottom); Valentyn Volkov, 6, 65 (foreground); volkovaa, 120; Katherine Welles, 13; Cameron Whitman, 158; Wollertz, 166; Scott Wong, 185; Robert Wroblewski, 162; zcw, 176 (bottom); Slawomir Zelasko, 28; Zheltyshev, 61; Zhukov Oleg, 154

Flickr:
Matthew Beckler, 115 (bottom); ben+sam, 107; BLACKDAY, 124; brettanomyces, 96; Andrew Chellinsky, 37 (top); choking sun, 94 (bottom), 99 (right); Jason Cipriani, 92; Wheeler Cowperthwaite, 95; Paul Downey, 79 (top); ilovebutter, 53 (bottom), 63, 64 (top), 101, 105, 128; Joe Lipson, 56; Daniel Lobo, 26 (inset), 49, 99 (left), 100; Tim Marshall, 42 (bottom), 98; Mat the WFLK, 43, 54 (top and bottom), 67; Craige Moore, 51; Paco Lyptic, 97; Tim Patterson, 55 (top); Colby Perry, 34, 38, 129 (top); Daniel Spiess, 60; steve sparks, 52; surfstyle, 123; terren in Virginia, 62 (bottom); trenttsd, 37 (bottom); Will, 53 (top); J_Wynia, 50

Additional contributors:
Frank Barickman, 139; Brewer's Friend (www.brewersfriend.com), 116 (top); Gina Cioli/i-5 Studio, 115 (top), 152; Kevin Fogle, 18, 19 (top), 20, 36, 39 (bottom), 44 (top), 48, 55 (bottom), 64 (bottom), 66, 104; Fiona Green, 8, 141, 184, 186 (top), 187, 188, 189; Cory Hershberger, 111; Daniel Johnson, 193 (top), 194 (bottom); Patricia Lenhardt, 190, 191, 195, 196, 197, 198; Library of Congress, 12 (inset), 15 (inset); James McNulty, 138; Sheila Nielsen, 136; Andrea Ratulowski, 181 (top), 182, 183; Terry Wild, 19 (bottom), 73 (bottom)

About the Editor

Cory Hershberger lives in Lexington, Kentucky, and is the associate editor for *Hobby Farms* and *Chickens* magazines. An avid cat lover, book devourer, and home brewer, Cory operates Mother Hen Brewing with his friend Dustin and has made it his mission in life to try craft beer from all fifty states. Find him online at **www.coryhersh.com** and on Twitter at @zeecorster.